THE COMPLETE BEGINNER'S GUIDE TO MICROSCOPES AND TELESCOPES

Aaron E. Klein

THE COMPLETE
BEGINNER'S GUIDE TO
Microscopes AND Telescopes

DOUBLEDAY & COMPANY, INC. / GARDEN CITY, NEW YORK

Library of Congress Cataloging in Publication Data

Klein, Aaron E
  The complete beginner's guide to microscopes and telescopes.

  (The Complete beginner's guide series)
  Bibliography: p.
  Includes index.
  SUMMARY: Discusses the development of microscopes and telescopes,
how they work, and how to select and use them.
  1. Microscope and microscopy—Juvenile literature.
2. Telescope—Juvenile literature. [1. Microscope and microscopy,
2. Telescope] I. Title
QH278.K45   502'.8'2

Library of Congress Catalog Card Number 78-22334

ISBN: 0-385-14854-2
ISBN: 0-385-14855-0

9 8 7 6 5 4 3 2

Contents

The Big and the Small-
The Near and the Far

What do you know about microscopes and telescopes? If nothing else, you probably know that microscopes are used to make small things look bigger, and telescopes are used to make things that are far away seem to be closer. Those are certainly among the many uses of microscopes and telescopes. But what do you know about the ideas of big and small? Far and near?

Look at yourself in a mirror. Are you big? Are you small? I'm a pretty big kid, you might say, or you might say, I'm a little kid but that's O.K. because I'll grow. On the other hand, you might be overweight. In that case, you might wish you weren't so big. Or it could be that you don't think of yourself as either big or little. Up to this time, you may have considered yourself to be medium, sort of middle-sized.

Think about those words "big," "little," and "medium" for a minute. There is something about those words that seems to hang loose. Let's try to find out what it is.

Suppose you are in the sixth grade. Sixth-graders are generally around eleven years old. Some might be twelve or more, others might be ten. Sixth-graders come in all sizes. Say the biggest kid in the class is five feet three inches tall and weighs around 115 pounds and the smallest kid is three feet eleven inches tall and weighs around 80 pounds. Now imagine that you are four feet ten inches tall and weigh 95 pounds. What do you think about your own size now? Are you big, small, or medium? Is this judgment of yourself a little different from what it was when you were by yourself and looked at yourself in the mirror?

If you spend most of your time hanging around the biggest kid in your class, you might start to feel a little undersized. If it bothers you, and there's no reason that it should, take a walk down the hall to the kindergarten. There is nothing like all those little kindergarten kids to make a person feel big and mighty. But if you think you felt small next to the biggest kid in class, think how he or she would feel standing next to the defensive front four of the Los Angeles Rams. The biggest kid in the sixth grade might not feel so big anymore.

By now you may be thinking that the word "big," "small," and "medium" don't mean too much standing by themselves. If that's what you are thinking, you are absolutely right. Big, small, and medium mean absolutely nothing unless you are comparing one or more things to another. Compared to the kindergarten kids, you are big; compared to the biggest kid in class, you are a bit on the small side. On the other hand, that biggest kid in class looks pretty runty standing up to the Los Angeles Rams defensive line. And the biggest guy on the football team is less than puny compared to a blue whale, the largest animal in the world.

Hey, wait a minute, you might say. When I am all by myself, I know that I am big, small, or medium. But if you stop to think about it again, even if you are not aware of it, you are always comparing yourself to other things and people you have seen. This kind of comparing goes for any object. You would have no way of knowing, for example, that a basketball is a big ball unless you have compared it to a baseball or a ping-pong ball.

Kids in the sixth grade and football players, basketballs and ping-pong balls have one important thing in common. You can see them and tell what they are with your eyes alone. Your eyes need no help to make out what they are. But there is much in this world and out of it that you cannot see clearly or perhaps not see at all with just your eyes alone.

Let's consider an all too familiar object — a mosquito. Compared to yourself, a mosquito is very, very small. You may have heard some tall tales about huge, mean, vicious mosquitoes.

However, the meanest, most vicious, and biggest mosquitoes in the world are tiny indeed compared to you. If you weigh ninety pounds, it would take about 580,000 of these mosquitoes to weigh as much as you do. If you are five feet tall, about three hundred of the most common type of mosquitoes, stacked end to end, would be needed to make a tower of mosquitoes as tall as you.

These numbers make a mosquito seem pretty small. But can a mosquito ever be thought of as being big? You had better believe it. There is, for example, a living thing called a *Colpidium*. (You would be quite likely to see one if you examined pond water with a microscope.) Let's not say how big it is in terms of inches, millimeters, or some other measurement. Let's simply compare a *Colpidium* to a mosquito. It would take about 5000,000 *Colpidia* to weigh as much as one mosquito. About 120 *Colpidia* stretched end to end would be needed to equal the length of one mosquito.

So it would seem that a *Colpidium* is about the smallest thing there is. Think again. There are bacteria so small that thousands of them wouldn't weigh as much as one *Colpidium*.

Are bacteria the smallest living things around? Not at all. Viruses, for example, the things that cause common colds and flu, are tiny, tiny compared to bacteria. Then there are atoms and molecules. As you probably know, everything you, the mosquito, this book, the floor or chair you are sitting on — *everything* is made of molecules. Molecules are made of atoms, the basic "building blocks" of everything there is. How small are molecules? That depends on how many atoms are in the molecule. Some molecules have only two atoms while others have millions of atoms in them. But even the biggest of molecules, containing tens of millions of atoms, cannot be seen with your eye alone. And even the most powerful of microscopes can just barely make the largest molecules visible.

Atoms come in different sizes, too, but the difference in size between the smallest and largest molecules is insignificant compared to the differences between sizes in molecules. The largest natural atom is the uranium atom. The smallest atom is the hydrogen atom. An uranium atom weighs about 238 times as much as a hydrogen bomb. There are atoms larger than uranium, but these atoms were made in laboratories by scientists.

Scientists make elements by adding neutrons to the element. One of the best-known man-made elements is **plutonium,** the raw material of atomic bombs. It seems that atoms are about the smallest things around. They certainly are small compared to you and compared to everything you can see and much of what you can't see. But atoms are made up of smaller parts. These parts have names such as electrons, protons, mesons, neutrons. These parts are made of even smaller particles. What, then, is the smallest thing in the world or in the universe? No one knows the answer to that question yet. Almost every year, scientists discover even smaller atomic particles, and no one yet knows what the end to that search will be.

Let's look in the other direction now. Think about the word "far." Far is a word used to describe distance. Like big and small, "far" is a comparative term. "Far" means something only when compared to "near" or "close." You might have gone to a football game in one of the bigger stadiums and sat on the top row or near the top row. For the money you paid, you probably thought you were pretty far away from the action on the field. The players may have looked like little dolls or, even worse, like little insects. Compared to the people sitting in the first row, you certainly were far away from the field, but if you compare the actual distance between the top row of the stadium and the playing field, it might seem rather short compared to how far you walked on a hike or the distance you walk or ride to school every day (unless you live next door or across the street from the school). Or if your car runs out of gas two miles from the nearest gas station, that two miles will seem like an awfully long distance, but in an automobile, on a motorcycle or even a bicycle that two miles would not seem so long.

We often think of distance in terms of time. That is, if someone asks how far it is to the next town we might answer, "a thirty-minute drive." Frequently, however, the time is more related to traffic conditions and how crowded the area is than to the actual distance. To travel a mile by automobile in New York City could take an hour or longer in bad traffic. But the same mile could be traveled on an expressway in about a minute. A jet airliner can travel ten miles in about a minute and a half (about 600 miles an hour). While ten miles is an insignificant distance for a jet airplane, that distance can be very important if that is how far you have to travel in an automobile in heavy traffic to get to the airport in time to catch the plane.

Let's assume that the airliner is traveling at a speed of 600 miles an hour. At that speed, the airplane can travel the 3,000 miles from New York to San Francisco in about five hours. Three thousand miles could certainly be considered to be far. It is far compared to the distance between your school and your home and compared to the distance between the top row of the stadium and the playing field.

The Moon is about 256,000 miles away from the Earth (the distance varies according to where the Moon is in its orbit). At 600 miles an hour it would take about eighteen days to reach the Moon. The Moon may not seem very far away, however. After all, people have been to the Moon and back and, in this age of fast travel, the distance may not seem too great. But walking 256,000 miles would certainly impress upon you the idea of great distance.

The Sun, however, is another matter. The Sun is about 93 million miles away from the Earth. If you traveled toward the Sun at 600 miles an hour it would take about eighteen *years* to get there. Far, far indeed.

But the Sun is a close neighbor compared to other stars (yes, the Sun is a star). The closest star other than the Sun is called Proxima Centauri. At 600 miles an hour it would take over 480,000 years to get there. That seems far, but remember Proxima Centauri is the nearest star other than the Sun. There are stars within our own star system, or galaxy, that would take millions of years to reach at the speed of a jet airplane. And then there are galaxies beyond our own galaxy. The closest galaxy to our own is so far away that to talk about how long it would take to get there at 600 miles an hour results in a number that is practically impossible to comprehend: 5,479,400,000,000,000,000 years, give or take a few million. Can you read that number? Written out, the number is five septillion, four hundred and seventy-nine quintillion, four hundred quadrillion years. And compared to other galaxies, that galaxy is a near neighbor to our own.

We have talked about the very small and the very far. The very far and the very small are a new world that you can discover with microscopes and telescopes. Before there were microscopes, people did not know — indeed they could not know — of the existence of very small things such as bacteria and *Colpidia*. They certainly knew about mosquitoes, but they could not know about how marvelously complicated a mosquito was. Without a way to enlarge their view of the mosquito, people could not see the hundreds of hairs and bristles, the beautifully complicated eyes, and the other little details of how a mosquito is put together.

Before there were telescopes, people could not know what stars really were nor could they know how far away they really were. They could not know that the Moon was covered with mountains and craters. Of course, people could see the stars without a telescope. Among the stars they saw were those they called *asteres planetes* — wandering stars. These were what are called planets, today. Without the help of telescopes people could not see that these *asteres planetes* were different from the other stars. For one thing, they moved through the skies while the stars seemed to stay in one place. They were also brighter than most of the other stars. Without telescopes, however, people could not see that the planets were not stars at all. Without telescopes they could not see the many-colored bands on Jupiter or the rings around Saturn, and without telescopes people could not know there were other planets beyond the five that were known before telescopes were available (Mercury, Venus, Mars, Jupiter, and Saturn).

What about Earth, you might ask? Didn't people know that the Earth was a planet? The answer to that question is that they did not know. Until about three hundred and fifty years ago, most people, including scholars, scientists, and educated people, believed that the Earth was the center of the universe. That is, it was believed that the stars, the Sun, the Moon, the planets, everything that could be seen in the skies, revolved about the Earth.

The idea that the Earth is not the center of the universe, that the Earth revolved about the Sun, as do the other planets, was proposed before there were telescopes. A Polish astronomer named Nicolaus Copernicus (ko-PURR-nick-us) proposed the idea that the Earth was not the center of the universe. He was certainly not the first astronomer to so believe, but he was the first to make this idea well known. He proposed the idea in a book he wrote in 1543. Copernicus was only one of many astronomers who did their work before there were telescopes. The evidence of his idea of the **heliocentric universe** ("helio" means sun and "centric" refers to center; "heliocentric universe" means sun-in-the-center) came from mathematical calculations. The Sun is not actually the center of the universe. It is the center of the solar system which is the Sun and the planets that move around the Sun.

There are also asteroids and comets. Asteroids are chunks of rock varying in size from pebbles to chunks several miles thick and long. They are found between the orbits of Mars and Jupiter and are thought to be the remains of a planet that broke apart billions of years ago. Comets swing around the Sun in wide, oddly shaped orbits. They are made of frozen gases and other materials.

What was seen with the help of telescopes helped to convince people that Copernicus was right. A scientist named Galileo Galilei agreed with Copernicus after he used a telescope to see moons spinning around Jupiter. You may have heard somewhere along the line that Galileo invented the telescope. Galileo did not invent the telescope but, in 1610, he did make use of one of the earliest. He was one of the first, if not the very first person, to make serious observations with the instrument.

The idea that the Earth was not the center of the universe was not exactly an instant success. The other idea—that everything in the heavens revolved around the Earth—had been part of human thought for over two thousand years and people were comfortable with it. On the other hand, the thought that the Earth was only a tiny speck in a vast, endless universe frightened many people and they did not want to believe it.

At about the same time that Galileo made his telescope, the earliest microscopes were made. While telescopes helped people to find out more about other worlds, microscopes helped people to find out about beautiful worlds right here. It would not be wrong to say that this world was right under their noses. People saw tiny living things that no one could have ever dreamed of before the microscope showed they existed. Ordinary things like grains of salt and the wings of flies became breathtaking views of beauty. The grains of salt appeared to be glittering jewels and a fly's wing became a gossamer landscape crisscrossed with rivers.

The microscope has helped to find out more about the world we live in than any other instrument. With the help of microscopes, the causes of many diseases were discovered. Once the causes were determined, ways to cure or prevent these diseases could be found. The microscopes helped to find out some very important things about life. For example, without microscopes we could not have known that all living things are made of cells. You can see some of your own cells with a microscope. The microscope is still one of the most important tools used by scientists.

One of the first people to make good use of microscopes was a Dutchman named Anton van Leeuwenhoek (LAY-van-hook). He was not the inventor of the microscope, although many people think so. But he was one of the first to report on what he saw.

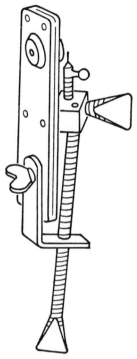

An artist's version of a Leeuwenhoek microscope. The object to be observed was put on the sharp point under the metal plate. The microscope was brought right up to the eye.

He saw tiny animals in a drop of water and he called them "cavorting beasties." Some ten years earlier, an Englishman named Robert Hooke wrote a book about what he had seen with his microscope. The book was filled with drawings of his observations. You may have heard that all living things are made of cells. Hooke was the first person to use the word "cell" in that sense. He examined a piece of cork under the microscope. In his book, Hooke said he had sliced the cork "exceeding thin." He described how the cork seemed to be made of many tiny boxes or "cells." Actually, Hooke was not looking at living cells. He was looking at the remains of dead cells. What he saw, however, led to the knowledge that all living things are made of cells.

Today, for not too much money, you can buy or make a telescope that is better in every respect than Galileo's telescope. With a small, inexpensive telescope you can see the mountains and craters on the Moon, the moons of Jupiter and many other wondrous, beautiful things in the sky. In fact, on a clear night you can see the moons of Jupiter with a pair of binoculars. And with a relatively inexpensive microscope, you can see the little tufts, hairs, and barbs on a mosquito, and many other fascinating things. Microscopes and telescopes opened up a whole new world for scientists hundreds of years ago. They can do the same for you.

MEASURING

Just saying that something is "very small" or "very far away" is usually not enough information. Most of the time, you will want a measurement of some kind. Measurement, however, is really nothing more than comparing.

For example, chances are that if anyone every asks you about your size, they won't ask, "How big are you?"; they will ask something like, "How much do you weigh?" or "How tall are you?" If you wanted to, you could answer, "I am 600 mosquitoes tall." "I weigh 600,000 mosquitoes." That kind of measurement might mean something to you if you knew the weight and length of mosquitoes, but it wouldn't mean a great deal to anyone who was not familiar with the "mosquito measurement system."

Many different kinds of measurement systems have been around for a long time. These measurement systems were made by people to suit their needs. There are measurement systems for many things, such as buying and selling everyday needs, as well as for working with microscopes and telescopes. If any measurement is going to mean anything, it has to be based on a system that everyone concerned knows. You could make up your own system for measuring if you wanted to. Put your index finger down on a piece of paper. Put a mark on the paper where the finger joins the hand and another where the finger ends. You now have a **unit of measurement.** What are you going to call this unit of measurement? You could call it a "finger" since that is what it is, a finger of measure. Or you could give it a more interesting name such as goonymander, pletzl, or veeck, or whatever pleases you.

Let's say you picked "goonymander" as the name of your unit. Is the "goonymander" useful for all measurements you might care to make? Suppose you wanted to measure your height in "goonymanders." You could, you know. You can make a "goonymander ruler" by marking off a stick in "goonymander" units and then holding it up to yourself. How many "goonymanders" tall are you?

But suppose you wanted to measure the length of the soccer or football field at school. The "goonymander" is not particularly convenient for that purpose. It is too small. Similarly, it would be very inconvenient to try to measure the distance between Chicago and Omaha, for example, in "goonymanders." You would need a bigger unit to conveniently measure something the length of a soccer field. So you can invent some more units. You could, for example, say that eight "goonymanders" equal a "kritz" (or whatever you care to call it), and that fourteen "kritzes" equal a "lumph," and that twenty-nine "lumphs" are one "heggelstan." Quick! How many "kritzes" are in a "heggelstan"?

After getting some practice with your system, you might get to be comfortable with it. That is, after you have learned how many "goonymanders" are in a "kritz" and how many "lumphs" are in a "heggelstan" and so on. But is the system of any use to anyone but you? Suppose you wanted to buy some rope. If you went to the hardware store and asked for twelve kritzes of rope, you might get some curious stares and perhaps a "beg pardon?" or two, but you are not likely to get rope by the kritz.

Suppose you wanted to measure the length of a mosquito with your system. Place a mosquito alongside your goonymander ruler and you will see that you have a problem. A goonymander is so much longer than a mosquito that the length of the mosquito would have to be expressed as a fraction, and a rather small fraction at that.

The goonymander system is a way to measure length but length is not all there is to be measured. There is volume and there is mass, or weight. Volume is how much space something takes up. The unit of volume you are probably most familiar with is the quart. Mass is how much of something there is, and weight is how much the gravity of the Earth pulls on that something. The unit of mass or weight you are most familiar with is the pound.

Many people are confused by the words **mass** and **weight.** As far as most of us are concerned, mass and weight are the same thing. There are situations, however, in which they can be different. As long as you stay on the surface of the Earth your mass and weight are the same. Suppose, however, you go out into space. Your mass will be unchanged (assuming you don't lose any), but your weight will change. You will weigh nothing in space because there is no gravity.

Now pounds, quarts, feet, inches, and yards are units you know something about. A request for twelve yards of rope will get you the merchandise. But where did these units come from? They had to be invented by someone, somewhere, sometime. These familiar units came about in much the same way as the kritz and the goonymander. An inch was based on the distance between the end of the thumb and the first joint on the hand of the King. This kind of measurement was fine for England. It was also fine in places that Englishmen went to, such as the colonies in North America that became the United States. But it wasn't used anywhere else. Other places had their own systems of measurement used for local trade. When it came to trading with other countries, however, one country's local system of measurement was no better than goonymanders, kritzes, and heggelstans in another country. Some units, such as barrels and hogsheads, became more or less international units, but, in general, the situation was a mess.

A better way to measure things was needed. So, in 1791, a group of scientists in France got together to make a better way. Science, as we know it today, was just getting started in those days. There was a need for an accurate standard of measurement that scientists all over the world could use. The system of measurement devised in France in 1791 is still used in most of the world today. It is called the **metric system.** The United States is the only major country in the world in which the people still do not use the metric system for ordinary measuring, buying, selling, and so on. However, scientists in the United States use the metric system.

There are three basic units of measurement in the metric system. They are the meter for length; the gram for mass; and the liter for volume. Let's concentrate on the meter, since length is the measurement you will be most concerned with when you use a microscope or telescope. The handy thing about the metric system is that units are all based on ten. All you have to remember is multiples of ten. This method is a lot easier than remembering many different units, such as that 16 ounces make a pint, or that 12 inches make a foot, or that 3 feet make a yard, and so on.

You can get an idea of the size of metric units by taking a look at a metric ruler or meterstick. A meterstick is like a yardstick except that it measures a meter and not a yard. Take a look at the smallest division on that meterstick. That is a **millimeter.** A millimeter is 1/1000 of a meter. If you are still thinking in the old system, it takes about twenty-five millimeters to make an inch. Many people think of an inch as a pretty small unit of measurement, but compared to a millimeter an inch is pretty big. Try measuring our friend the mosquito in terms of inches and you have a problem. But the millimeter is handy for measuring something the size of a mosquito. You don't have to bother with all those tricky fractions.

Now suppose you wanted to measure a *Colpidium* (remember that about 120 *Colpidia* stretched end to end would equal the length of one mosquito). A millimeter is suddenly not so handy anymore. When people started using microscopes and they saw little things such as *Colpidia* and bacteria, it didn't take them long to realize that if they wanted to measure things that small, a millimeter was big and clumsy. They needed a smaller unit and one was invented to meet the need. That unit is the **micron.** A micron is, if you can imagine, one 1/1000 of a millimeter. Now that's small! You would think that a micron (about 1/25,000 of an inch) is about as small a measure of length as one might need. Think again. Later in this book we will talk about a kind of microscope called the electron microscope. This microscope has enabled people to see things so small that in measuring them, the micron becomes much more clumsy than using an inch to measure a mosquito. So, still another unit was devised to deal with this world of smallness. This unit is called an **Angstrom.** An Angstrom is 1/10,000 of a micron.

Astronomers also need special units of measurement. As better and better telescopes began to help people to see things farther and farther away, it soon became obvious that units such as miles and kilometers (a kilometer is 1,000 meters) were clumsy to use for measuring distances to stars and galaxies. Remember Proxima Centauri, the star other than the Sun that is closest to Earth? We talked about its distance from the Earth in terms of how long it would take to get there at 600 miles an hour. Suppose you wanted to know the actual distance to Proxima Centauri in terms of some unit of measurement of length. What kind of unit would you pick? A big one, certainly. What are some of the big units of length you might know? Let's try miles. In miles, the approximate distance from Earth to Proxima Centauri is 25,-777,980,000,000 miles. That's 25 trillion, 777 billion, 980 million miles. That is a ridiculously large number to have to use. If you try to describe this distance in kilometers the number would be still larger, because a kilometer is a smaller unit than a mile. And remember that we are talking about the *closest* star other than the Sun.

One of the most widely used units of measurement in astronomy is the light-year. Using the light-year is much like our use of a speed measurement to get across the idea of distance. A light-year is the distance that light travels in one year. You may, or may not, know that light travels very fast. There is nothing known that moves faster than light. The speed of light is about 186,282 miles per second (299,792 kilometers per second). A light-year is equivalent to almost 6 trillion miles (5.8786 trillion miles, to be a bit more exact, or 9.4607 trillion kilometers). It is easy to see that the light-year is much handier to use than a mile or kilometer to measure distances to the stars. The distance to Proxima Centauri, for example, is 4.3 light-years. It doesn't sound so far away expressed in light-years, does it? Well, compared to galaxies that are *billions* of light-years away, Proxima Centauri is a neighbor within hailing distance.

There are other units besides the light-year for use in measuring astronomical distances. One of these is the *astronomical unit* (A.U.). An astronomical unit is the average distance between the Earth and the Sun. It is equivalent to 149,597,910 kilometers or 92,955,832 miles. The A.U. is handy to use when considering distances between planets in the solar system. The light-year is a bit too big, and miles and kilometers are hopelessly clumsy.

Another widely used unit of measurement is the *parsec*. The parsec is equivalent to 3.2616 light-years. It is used to measure the great distances between galaxies. The parsec is based on the distance at which the Earth and Sun would seem, to an observer, to be one second of an arc apart. An *arc* is a part or segment of a circle. A circle is measured in degrees. There are 360 degrees in a circle. A degree is divided into 60 minutes and a minute is divided into 60 seconds. The expression "five seconds of arc" would describe the size of an arc or circle segment. Just how much actual distance that represents depends on how big the circle is. The farther away you are from two points, the closer together they seem to be in terms of sections of an arc. Microns, Angstroms, light-years, astronomical units, and so on, are measurements that belong to other worlds—the world of the very small and the very far. These are worlds you can explore with microscopes and telescopes.

What Are Microscopes and Telescopes — How Do They Work?

You may have already used a microscope even if you never owned or borrowed one. That certainly sounds odd. How can you have used something if you have never had or even borrowed it? But have you ever used a magnifying glass? If so, you have used a kind of microscope. Although a magnifying glass is probably not what you have in mind when you think of a microscope, it does many of the same things a microscope does. A magnifying glass is also a kind of telescope.

A magnifying glass, a microscope, and a telescope have certain things in common. The basic thing they all have in common is *lenses*. A magnifying glass is a lens, and microscopes and telescopes are, basically, combinations of lenses.

Lenses

You may think of a lens as something that makes whatever you are looking at seem bigger. That is certainly what a magnifying glass does, and a magnifying glass is, indeed, a lens. Lenses do certain things to light and, in so doing, lenses can make small things appear to be bigger and things far away seem to be closer. Lenses and light — that's what microscopes and telescopes are all about. Before we say much more about lenses, it might be a good idea to say a few things about light.

What almost everybody knows about light is that light is what enables us to see. What you may not know is that light travels in straight lines from whatever it is that is producing the light. Most of the light we see comes from the Sun. Light travels in straight lines through all those millions of miles (93 million miles) of space between the Sun and the Earth. Light also travels in straight lines from a light bulb, a flashlight, candle, firefly, or from whatever else produces light.

Light does not always travel in straight lines, however. Light can be bent when it passes from one kind of thing to another. You know that light passes through some things and not through others. Light passes through space and it passes through air. You know that light passes through most kinds of glass.

Whatever it is that light passes through is called the **medium.** Now, when light passes *at an angle* from one medium to another medium of a different thickness, the light is bent. When the light from the Sun passes from space into the atmosphere around the Earth, the light is bent because the atmosphere of Earth is thicker than space.

When light passes from air into glass it is certainly passing from one medium to another. Ordinarily, glass is made so that it bends light as little as possible. After all, when you look through a window you want to get a natural view. Sometimes, however, window glass does bend the light a bit. Sometimes things look peculiar when viewed through glass that is not of very good quality. Things may look "wiggly" when viewed through such glass. This effect is particularly noticeable if you move your head up and down or from side to side when you are looking through the glass. The peculiar look is caused by the bending of the light. Another word for this bending is *refraction*. The way that lenses *refract* light is what makes microscopes and telescopes useful.

Most lenses are made of glass. Some are made of plastic, but whatever they are made of they must be clear, that is, transparent. Lenses are made in different shapes. A piece of cheap glass in a windowpane can be a bother and a nuisance, but a piece of glass shaped into a lens can be a source of joy and wonder.

How did people find out about lenses? Like many of the other great discoveries, lenses were discovered accidentally. No one person actually discovered lenses. People found out about them slowly over many hundreds of years. One of the first steps toward the making of lenses was the discovery of glass. Again,

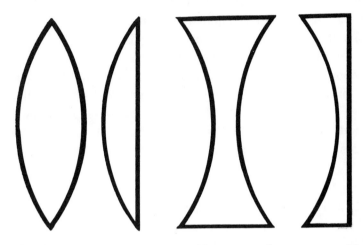

Types of lenses. From left to right: biconcave, planoconcave, biconvex, planoconvex.

no one knows who first found out how to make glass, but it is known that Egyptians were making glass as early as 1500 B.C. Around 800 B.C., a people called the Phoenicians (fuh-NEE-shuns) had established a thriving glass business. They learned how to blow glass into beautiful shapes. The Phoenicians were also good sailors, and their ships carried glass vases, goblets, cups, and other items to ports in Greece, Rome, and other places along the Mediterranean Sea. By 100 B.C., the Romans had conquered all the lands around the Mediterranean Sea, and the Phoenicians no longer existed as a separate people. Their ideas of glassblowing, however, were eagerly adopted by the Romans and they soon became highly skilled at fashioning glass into beautiful objects.

Many of the glass objects made by Roman craftsmen were designed to hold water. Some were used as flower vases. Others were just meant to be admired. It did not take long for people to notice that when you looked at something through a water-filled goblet of a certain shape, whatever it was you were looking at seemed to be bigger. A Roman philosopher. Seneca, wrote, in A.D. 65, that glass jars filled with water were useful for seeing things "that frequently escape the eye."

Over the next several hundred years, many scientists and mathematicians studied how goblets of water and glass, curved into particular shapes, could bend light and change the way things seemed to be. By the 1300s, eyeglasses had been invented. The development of eyeglasses was a first step toward microscopes and telescopes.

Early Microscopes and Telescopes

The invention and use of spectacles came at around the same time that people in Europe started to get interested in science again. After the fall of the Roman Empire, Europe went into a decline that historians have called the Dark Ages. People had very little time to devote to art, science, or much of anything else beyond their basic needs. Practically all science — what there was of it — was in the Arab countries. Slowly, however, as conditions improved, there was more time to think about art and science.

Science, as we think of science today, started to grow around the 1600s. Science is an organized way to find out whatever there is to find out about the world and universe in which we live. To do all this finding-out, we have to use our senses: seeing, hearing, smelling, touching, and so on. The early scientists soon found out that eyes, ears, and noses alone were not always enough. You could see a flea, for example, but if you wanted to find out more about how the flea was put together you needed something more than just your eyes. That "something" was available in the form of magnifying glasses. By the 1500s, the art of grinding glass into lenses was fairly highly developed, especially in Holland. Dutch lens makers were regarded as the best. You could, if you had the money, buy a special kind of lens called a *flea microscope* from Dutch lens grinders. As you might have guessed, the flea microscope was designed primarily for examining fleas and other insects.

A single magnifying glass was still not enough. It was obvious that there was more to be seen, both far out in the heavens and among tiny things on our own planet, than could be seen with an ordinary magnifying glass. Somewhere along the way, someone found that by combining two or more lenses you could get more magnification and more seeing power. These combinations of lenses were the first microscopes and telescopes.

Just who made the very first microscope and the very first telescope is not known. From records that exist, it seems that the earliest microscopes and telescopes were made in the 1580s or 1590s. One of these was made by Hans and Zacharias Janssen, a father and son team, who ran a lens-grinding business in Middleburg, Holland. Not too much is known about the Janssen microscope other than that it was a metal tube with lenses placed at either end. Nor is it known if anyone ever bought one, or if anyone ever wrote down what he observed with it. The Janssen's microscope had more than one lens. As such, it was a *compound microscope*.

Starting in the early 1600s, more people started to make microscopes and telescopes. Few of these people went into the microscope and telescope business just for the joy of it. They expected to make money from selling their instruments. Then, as now, a smart businessman would not spend his time and money making a product unless there was a demand for it. There certainly was a demand for microscopes and telescopes in the 1600s. Although the demand was there, the microscope and telescope business was not what you would call "big business."

A reproduction of the Jannsen microscope. The original was made around 1590. *(Courtesy Bausch and Lomb Inc., Rochester, N.Y.)*

There were not microscopes and telescopes in every home as there are TV sets today. There were, however, enough educated, curious people around, who wanted these instruments and had the leisure time to use them.

Men (in the 1600s women were not supposed to be scientifically curious) who were interested in science formed societies or associations. The idea of these associations was to bring together these men so that they could share their experiences and learn from each other. One of the earliest of these societies was the Academy of the Lynx (*Academia dei Linci*) founded in Rome in 1601. The society was named for the lynx, a kind of wildcat that has very good eyesight. One of the main objectives of the group was to observe things in nature as closely as possible. These groups helped to create a demand for instruments such as microscopes and telescopes. The competition for this business served to speed up the improvement of these instruments. Galileo was an active participant in the activities of the Academy of the Lynx.

Another of these early societies was the Royal Society of England, founded in 1662. Robert Hooke was a member of the Royal Society. Robert Hooke worked with a compound microscope that had a magnifying power of about 30× (magnified 30 times). He did not limit his work to looking at cork. He observed insects, feathers, and much more. Although Hooke was not the first person to use a microscope, he was one of the first to keep detailed records of what he saw.

Another person who kept detailed records was Anton van Leeuwenhoek. Leeuwenhoek was a Dutch cloth merchant. Lens grinding and looking at things with his lenses was more or less a hobby with him. Leeuwenhoek microscopes were *simple microscopes*. That is, they consisted of one lens. The lens was mounted in a metal plate. The specimen was held on a needle-shaped mechanism just under the lens. To use the microscope, the plate had to be held very close to the eye. Leeuwenhoek did his work in the 1680s. The design of his microscope did not have much influence on microscopes that were built in later years.

Leeuwenhoek's tiny lenses could get more magnification than any other microscopes that were available in the late 1600s. Leeuwenhoek was probably the first person to see bacteria and the many other tiny living things that can be seen only with a microscope.

Leeuwenhoek would not tell anybody how he made his remarkable little lenses, but he was not so reluctant to tell the world what he saw. He wrote letters to the Royal Society in which he described his observations in great detail.

At about the same time the Janssens made their microscope, the first telescopes were being made. Galileo made his telescope in 1610. Galileo's telescope was a tube with a lens at either end. You may have noticed a similarity between the Janssen's microscope and Galileo's telescope. Both were tubes with lenses at either end. What, then, is the difference between a microscope and a telescope?

How Microscopes and Telescopes Work

Basically, a compound microscope and telescope are the same thing. At one end of the tube — the end away from the user — is the lens, called the objective lens (also called *object glass,* particularly in telescopes). The objective lens gathers the light from what you are looking at and brings it to a *focus* and forms an *image.* At the other end of the tube is a lens called the *eyepiece* or *ocular.* This lens is well named because it is the lens through which the observer looks with his or her eye.

What do we mean by *focus* and *image?* You can find out for yourself if you have a lens. You will also need a sunny day and a piece of white paper or cardboard and a measuring stick of some kind such as a meterstick, yardstick, or ruler. The best kind of lens to use is a not-too-strong eyeglass lens of the type used to correct farsightedness. Another lens you can use is the kind used on cameras to take close-up photographs. If you don't have any of those kinds of lenses, a magnifying glass will do.

Hold the lens and the paper so that you get a picture or *image* of the Sun on the paper. Move the lens back and forth until you get the sharpest image of the Sun on the paper or cardboard. DO NOT LOOK DIRECTLY AT THE SUN! LOOK AT THE PAPER. When the Sun is sharply focused on the paper, measure the distance between the lens and the paper. That distance is the *focal length* of the lens. This experiment works only with objects very far away, that is, at *infinity*. If you tried it with a close object such as a lamp or a light fixture, you would have seen an interesting image of the lamp or the light fixture on the piece of paper. The focal length, however, would vary depending on how far away the lamp is from the lens.

The focal length of the objective lens is the major difference between microscopes and telescopes. Telescope objective lenses have long focal lengths, while those of microscopes have short focal lengths. The lenses of telescopes are arranged to form images of things far away from the objective lens. The lenses of microscopes are designed to form images of things close to the objective lens. Objective lenses of telescopes are much larger than those of microscopes.

Galileo found that his telescope could be used as a microscope if the lenses were moved around a bit. Galileo's "microscope-telescope" and others like it were much too big to be used comfortably as a microscope. Some of these were so big you had to climb on ladders to use them.

We have been talking about one objective lens and one eyepiece lens for both microscopes and telescopes. Actually, modern microscopes and telescopes are made of many more than just two lenses. The various lenses are combined in different ways to give the best quality images.

Kinds of Telescopes

The type of telescope that Galileo built—an objective lens and an eyepiece lens—is called a *refracting telescope*. Most of the time, however, such telescopes are called simply *refractors*. They are called refractors because the lenses bend or refract the light to produce an image. When you think of a telescope, you may think first of how much it magnifies, that is, the *power* of the telescope. Power is important, but it is not the only thing about a telescope that is important. Of equal if not more importance than magnifying power is how much light the telescope gathers and the *resolving power* of the instrument.

Resolving power is the ability of the instrument to distinguish between two different points that are very close to each other. Stars are a good example, since stars are what you look at with a telescope. You see a star as a point of light in the sky. Many of the stars that you see as one star or one point of light, with your eyes alone, are actually two or more stars. However, the stars are so close together we see them as one star. (Remember that "far" and "close" are matters of comparison. From where we look at them, stars are close together. They could be millions of miles apart.) If you look at what seems to be one star through a telescope, and it is a good telescope with good resolving power, two stars will often show.

Resolving power is determined by the *aperture* (Ap-er-chur) of the object glass. The aperture is basically how wide the object glass is, that is, its diameter. The bigger the diameter, the more light-gathering power the telescope has and the better its resolving power is likely to be. The quality of the lens is another factor. A poor quality lens with a diameter of three inches might give poorer resolution than a high quality two-inch lens.

Magnification and resolving power are related to each other only in the fact that as magnification goes up resolving power

This refracting telescope has a 2-inch objective lens. *(Courtesy Unitron Instruments Inc., New Hyde Park, N.Y.)*

tends to go down. You can see this effect with a magnifying glass. With any magnifying glass there is a distance, between the object you are viewing and the magnifying glass, at which the sharpest image and best magnification are obtained. You can get more magnification, up to a point, by increasing the distance between the object and the glass but the image becomes blurred. You have increased the magnification but it is "empty" magnification, that is, it is magnification with no detail.

The magnifying power of a telescope is determined by the focal length of the objective. The longer the focal length, the more the magnification is likely to be. The object glass, however, is not the only set of lenses in the telescope. The eyepiece also figures in the total magnification obtained by the telescope. The total magnification of the telescope is obtained by dividing the focal length of the objective glass by the focal length of the eyepiece. So if you have a telescope that has an object glass with a focal length of 500 mm (millimeters) and an eyepiece with a focal length of 5 mm, the total magnification is 100 times, or as it is usually written, 100×.

You may have noticed a couple of things about magnification. One is that if you want to change the magnification, you change the eyepiece. An eyepiece with a focal length of 10 mm will give you a magnification of 50× if the focal length of the object glass is 500 mm. Another thing you may have noticed is that the shorter the focal length of the eyepiece the greater the total magnification. An eyepiece is somewhat like a microscope. It magnifies the image formed by the object glass. The eyepiece has the effect of bringing your eye closer to the image.

As the magnification gets higher, the field of view gets smaller. Say you are looking at a distant squirrel with your telescope. At 50×, for example, you might see the whole squirrel. At 300×, you might see only the squirrel's head, although the squirrel's head will appear to be bigger than it was at 50×. You will also notice that the squirrel is upside down. This is a characteristic of telescopes. They give you an upside down or **inverted** image. But you might know some people who have telescopes that give right-side-up images. Those telescopes have another set of lenses or prisms in them that turn the image right side up. That's fine, except that the extra lenses rob you of light. For each single lens or anything else that light passes through some light is lost. That's not too bad if you are looking at a squirrel. But if you are looking at a planet that is hundreds of millions of miles away, you want to get every possible bit of light from that planet through the telescope and into your eye. It doesn't make a bit of difference that the image of the planet is upside down. In space, the idea of upside down or right side up really doesn't matter. However, you do have to remember certain things such as the part of the planet that faces down in your telescope image is the North Pole and the part that seems "up" is the South Pole.

Reflecting Telescopes

Galileo and other telescope makers noticed something very disturbing about their telescopes. The disturbing thing was that the images they obtained with their instruments were ringed with haloes of color. While interesting to look at, and perhaps beautiful, these colors interfered with good observation. The reason for the color is to be found in the nature of light. Visible light is made up of all the colors of the rainbow or *spectrum.* As light passes from one medium to another it is not only bent but it also tends to break down into the colors of which it is made. You see this effect in a rainbow, but you see it more often in the spray from a garden hose. As the light passes through the droplets of water in the spray, it is broken down into colors.

The variously colored light came to a focus at different places in early telescopes, making it difficult to get a sharp focus. Early telescope makers found that they could cut down on this color effect (which is called *chromatic aberration* [kro-MA-tic ab-er-RAY-shun]) by using lenses of very long focal length. Longer

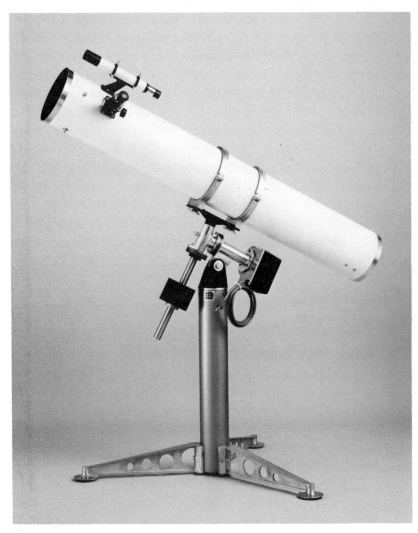

This reflecting telescope has a mirror six inches in diameter. *(Courtesy Meade Instruments Corporation, Inc., Costa Mesa, California)*

focal length object glasses were fine except that, in order to use them, the telescope tubes had to be very long. It is known that a telescope 200 feet long was made in the late 1600s, and one as long as 600 feet may have been made. These telescopes were almost useless. The slightest breeze would make them shake and shudder so much that the image bounced around. These telescopes, called "aerial" telescopes, could be used only when there was no wind at all.

Before refractors could be used in serious work by astronomers, the problems of chromatic aberration had to be beaten. The way to overcome it was shown in 1733 by Chester Moor Hall. Hall was an amateur scientist in England. There were quite a few of these "gentlemen scientists" in England in the 1700s. It was considered a fashionable thing to do for people of money and position. Most of them just played at science, but a few, such as Chester Moor Hall, made significant contributions to scientific work. Hall made an object lens out of two lenses. One lens was made of a kind of glass called *crown* and the other from glass called *flint*. The crown glass was not as thick (dense) as the flint glass. The light passed through the crown glass first and, as always, was broken up into colors. When the light passed through the flint glass, the colors were recombined into white light again. This kind of lens was called *achromatic* (AY-chro-MA-tic). Hall did not sell his new telescope, but a man named John Dolland, also an Englishman, began making achromatic telescopes in 1758.

Before achromatic lenses were invented, the clumsiness of the early refractors suggested that there had to be a better way. The better way was the **reflecting telescope.** A lens gathers and refracts light. A curved mirror also gathers light but it does not refract the light. It *reflects* the light. "Reflect" means "bounce," and that is what happens to light when it strikes a mirror. The light is bounced off the mirror at the same angle at which it hit the mirror.

As far as is known, the first reflecting telescope was made by one of the greatest, if not the greatest, of the early scientists, Sir Isaac Newton. This type of reflecting telescope is still widely used today and it is called, as you might expect, the Newtonian reflector. In the Newtonian reflector a curved mirror is placed at one end of an open tube. This mirror is called the *main mirror*. At the other end of the tube, but not quite at the end of it, there is a smaller mirror called the *flat*. Light is reflected from the main mirror onto the flat. The flat is placed at an angle so that light is reflected from it into the eyepiece. The user looks into the side of the telescope rather than into one end.

Since a mirror does not refract light, it does not break light down into its colors. The bothersome chromatic aberration was practically eliminated in reflectors. There was still a little from the eyepiece lenses, but early reflectors proved to be far more useful than early refractors.

Early reflectors suffered from a problem called *spherical aberration*. This kind of aberration occurs when the various light rays that strike the mirror do not come together in one point of focus. The result is a blurred image. Spherical aberration in a reflecting telescope mirror is corrected by deepening the curve in the central part of the mirror. Such a curve is called a *parabola*. Refractors have some spherical aberration too. It is corrected with additional lenses.

Newton's reflector had a mirror that was one inch in diameter. It was useless for any astronomical purpose, but it did show that a reflecting telescope was a possibility.

The bigger the diameter of the mirror, the better the resolution is likely to be. Just as a large lens will gather more light than a smaller lens, so will a large diameter mirror gather more light than a smaller diameter mirror. Like lenses, curved mirrors have focal lengths, and the longer the focal length the greater the magnification is likely to be.

While early reflectors overcame the problems of long, clumsy refractors, Newtonian reflectors can be bigger and clumsier than achromatic refractors with similar light-gathering and resolving power. For example, a refractor with a three-inch object lens can have as much if not more resolution and light-gathering power as does a reflector with a six-inch mirror. A six-inch mirror requires a tube at least seven inches in diameter and can be six feet long, or more. A telescope of that size would be much smaller than the "aerial" refracting telescopes of the 1600s, but it is considerably larger than a three-inch refractor. For someone who has to move a telescope to someplace where it can be used, size can be an important matter.

There are ways of designing reflectors to get the advantage of long focal length mirrors without lugging around tubes that look like sewer pipes. One such design is the *Cassegrain* (KASS-uh-grain) telescope. This type of telescope was invented by N. Cassegrain, a French astronomer, back in 1672. The Cassegrain reflector has achieved new popularity with amateur astronomers in recent years.

In a Cassegrain telescope, the light is collected by a main mirror as in a Newtonian reflector. The light is reflected to a secondary mirror as in a Newtonian. The secondary mirror in the Cassegrain is not flat as it is in the Newtonian. It is convex. The light from the secondary mirror is reflected back to the main mirror. There is a hole in the main mirror and the light passes through this hole and into an eyepiece. What the Cassegrain does is "fold" the focal length of the mirror into a shorter tube than would be required for a Newtonian reflector of similar focal length. Depending on the specific way the telescope is made, a Cassegrain telescope can have a focal length three to seven times as much as would be obtained using the same mirror in a Newtonian design.

The small size and compactness of Cassegrain telescopes are the main reasons for the popularity of these instruments.

A telescope similar to the Cassegrain is the *Maksutov*, invented by the Russian astronomer, Dmitri Maksutov, in 1944. The Maksutov is similar to the Cassegrain in that the main mirror has a hole in it through which light passes to the viewer.

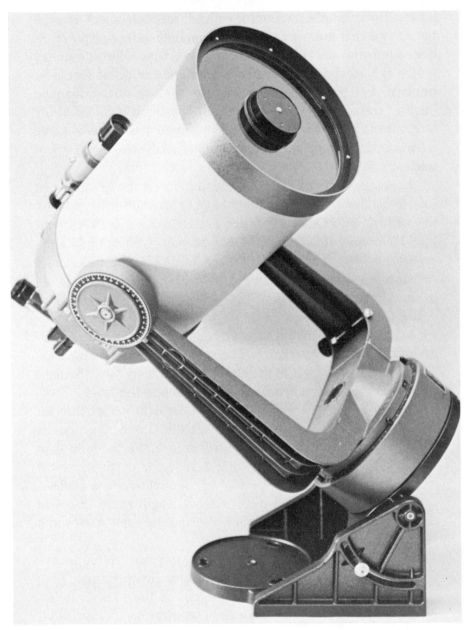

A Cassegrain reflecting telescope. (*Courtesy Celestron International, Torrance, California*)

A Maksutov reflecting telescope. *(Courtesy Celestron International)*

However, in the place of a small primary, there is something called the *Maksutov shell.* The Maksutov shell is a thick, steeply curved lens. The light passes through this lens before it reaches the mirror. In the center of the lens, however, there is a spot that reflects light. This spot acts somewhat as the secondary mirror of the Cassegrain and the Newtonian. The spot reflects the light back to the hole in the primary mirror and to the viewer. The Maksutov telescope, like the Cassegrain, is shorter than a Newtonian of the same focal length and combines some of the best features of lenses and mirrors.

Telescopes, by the way, are generally referred to by the diameter of the object lens or mirror. Therefore, a refracting telescope with a three-inch object lens would be called a three-inch refractor and a reflecting telescope with a six-inch mirror would be called a six-inch reflector.

The size and bulkiness of telescopes are mostly of concern to amateurs. Professional astronomers use huge telescopes which are kept in big domed buildings called observatories. Some serious amateurs also build observatories, but most people who use telescopes for a hobby have to be concerned with the size of the instruments. Most of them do not live in houses or apartments large enough to store huge telescopes comfortably. In general, however, as far as telescopes are concerned, bigger is better.

There are some big telescopes in use by astronomers today. Among the biggest are reflectors. At the Mount Wilson Observatory in California, there are a 60-inch reflector and a 100-inch reflector. Also in California, at Mount Palomar, is the famous 200-inch Hale reflector. This telescope is named for American astronomer Ellery Hale. Hale was responsible for persuading people with money to finance this and other big reflectors. The Hale was the largest reflector in the world until a 236-inch reflector was built in the Crimea Observatory in the Soviet Union.

There are also some big refractors in use. When glassmakers

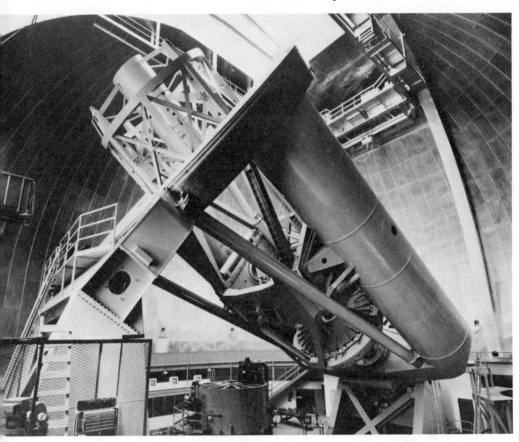

The 200-inch Hale Reflector at the Hale Observatory on Mount Palomar in California is the second largest reflecting telescope in the world. The primary mirror is at lower right. *(Courtesy Hale Observatories)*

perfected methods of making large glass disks around the early 1800s, the way was open to make larger refractors than had been made before. Some of the best and most famous of these refractors were made by an American firm, Alvan Clark and Sons. In the late nineteenth century they made a refractor with a 36-inch object lens and another with a 40-inch object lens. The 36-inch telescope is at the Lick Observatory in California and the 40-inch telescope is at the Yerkes Observatory in Wisconsin.

Why aren't there refractors that measure in the hundreds of inches as there are reflectors of that size? The problem is that refractor lenses have to be supported at the edges. If they are too wide, they will bend and wiggle. You can't put anything in the middle of them to support them because light has to pass all the way through the lens. Mirrors, on the other hand, can be supported all the way across the back.

The huge telescopes, particularly the big reflectors, are designed primarily to take pictures rather than to be looked through like a pair of binoculars or a small telescope. The "secondary mirror" of the 200-inch Hale telescope is so big that the operator sits inside its support while the telescope is being used. (The secondary is actually photographic film.) The big reflectors are used mostly to study deep space — that is, to study galaxies and other objects millions, and even billions, of light-years away.

Both reflectors and refractors are light-gathering instruments. As such they can be called *optical* instruments. (The study of light is called optics.) In recent years, however, another kind of telescope has been used to study deep space. This telescope is the radio telescope. Optical telescopes such as reflectors and refractors gather light given off from stars and other objects in space. Radio telescopes gather radio waves from stars, galaxies, and other bodies in space. The radio waves can often reveal more information about the space object than light can. These are not radio waves sent out by little green people from radio and television stations on distant planets. (Radio telescopes are capable of picking up such signals if they did exist.) But the radio

The 36-inch refractor at the Lick Observatory in California is the second largest refractor in the world. *(Courtesy Lick Observatory)*

The observer using the 200-inch Hale reflector sits in an observing cage inside the telescope. The main mirror can be seen below. *(Courtesy Hale Observatories)*

A radio telescope.

waves picked up by radio telescopes are natural radiation given off by stars and other bodies in space. Other telescopes gather X rays given off by the same sources.

Light and radio waves are energy in a form that is called *electromagnetic radiation*. There are many other kinds of this radiation such as X rays and ultraviolet light, to name only a few. This energy travels in straight lines, but the straight lines are in up and down waves. That is, they are up and down in relation to the direction in which the radiation is traveling. The only difference between light waves, radio waves, X rays, and so on is the length of the wave.

There are clouds of dust and other material in space that can block off the light from space objects. The radio waves and X rays can often get through the dust clouds. Picked up by radio telescopes and X-ray telescopes, these rays and waves can give scientists information that could not be obtained with optical telescopes.

Kinds of Microscopes

We have said before that microscopes and telescopes are basically the same kind of instrument. Like a telescope, a microscope has an object lens to gather light and an eyepiece, or ocular, to magnify the image formed by the object glass, or, as it is most often called in microscopes, the *objective*.

Early microscope makers were also troubled with chromatic aberration. The problem in microscopes has been solved in much the same way as it was for telescopes, by using combinations of lenses in the objective in order to eliminate the color.

Telescopes are designed to gather light from objects very far away. The lenses in microscopes, on the other hand, are designed to gather light from objects very close to the objective. As in telescopes, the eyepiece magnifies the image.

Resolving power in a microscope is a bit more complicated to explain than resolving power in a telescope. You will remember that the larger the objective lens, the better the resolving power of the telescope is likely to be. The objective lenses of microscopes are not very big. Compared to those of telescopes they are downright tiny. Microscopes, however, can achieve remarkably good resolution. That is, if the microscope is of good quality. The resolving power of the objective is determined by something called the **numerical aperture or** N.A. The N.A. is expressed as a number, such as 1.2. This number is engraved on the objectives of better microscopes. In general, the higher the N.A. the better the resolution.

The magnification you get with a microscope is found by multiplying the power of the objective by the power of the eyepiece. A look at the objective of most microscopes will reveal a number such as "10×" engraved on the objective. That means that the objective power has a magnifying power of 10. Now take a look at the eyepiece. There you will find another number such as "20×." Suppose you use a 20× objective with a 10× eyepiece. Multiplying 10 times 20 gives you 200, which is the magnifying power of the microscope with that eyepiece and that objective. The magnifying power would be written as 200×. On better-quality microscopes, you will also find the focal length of the objective written on the side. The focal length is expressed in millimeters.

A typical microscope is shown in the picture. This instrument is a light microscope. The word "light" does not refer to its weight but to the fact that it is light that passes into the lenses of the instrument and to the eye of the viewer. Not all microscopes are equipped with mirrors as is this one. Some have light sources built into the base. This mirror does not serve the same purpose as the mirror in a reflecting telescope.

Let's follow the path the light takes from the mirror or light source. From the mirror or light source the light passes through lenses in the **condenser.** The condenser concentrates the light. The condenser in this microscope is called a variable-focus con-

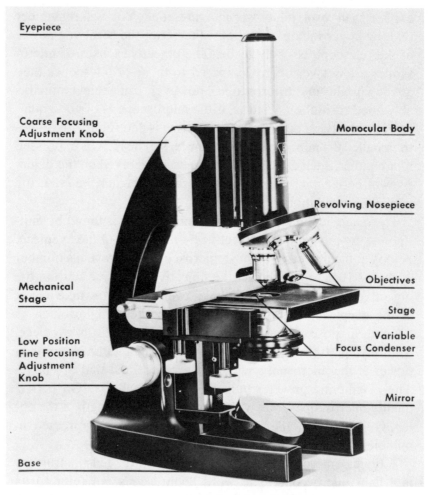

Eyepiece

Coarse Focusing
Adjustment Knob

Monocular Body

Revolving Nosepiece

Mechanical
Stage

Objectives

Stage

Low Position
Fine Focusing
Adjustment
Knob

Variable
Focus Condenser

Mirror

Base

A typical light microscope with some of the parts labeled. *(Courtesy Bausch and Lomb Optical Company, Rochester, N.Y.)*

denser because it can be moved up and down with a knob. Changing the focus of the condenser changes the nature of the light. The lens of the condenser fits into a hole in the **stage.** The stage is a flat, platformlike thing on which the specimen is placed. The specimen is what you want to examine with your microscope. The specimen is usually placed on a glass slide. This microscope is equipped with a **mechanical stage.** What that means is that the slide can be moved around on the stage by turning knobs rather than by moving the slide directly with your hands.

The light passes through the specimen and into the lenses of the objective. Notice that this microscope has three objectives. The **revolving nosepiece** is called that because it can be turned around to bring another objective into place. Changing to another objective raises or lowers the magnification depending on the power of the objective. The light then passes through the body of the instrument into the eyepiece.

There are two focusing knobs on this microscope — the **coarse adjustment** and the **fine adjustment.** The coarse adjustment moves the body up and down to get the objective in the right place for the sharpest image. The fine-adjustment knob does the same thing except that it does so in very small distances. It is used to bring the image into sharpest focus and to change the focus slightly in order to see things more sharply at different levels of the specimen. The fine adjustment could be compared to the fine-tuning knob on a TV.

We said that the light passes through the specimen. It might seem to you that the specimen would have to be very thin in order for light to pass through it, and you are absolutely right. Specimens viewed with this kind of microscope must be very thin indeed, that is, practically transparent. You will remember that Robert Hooke sliced the cork "exceeding thin." Other types of microscopes are designed to examine thicker specimens through which light does not pass at all. In this kind of microscope the light is directed on to the specimen rather than through it.

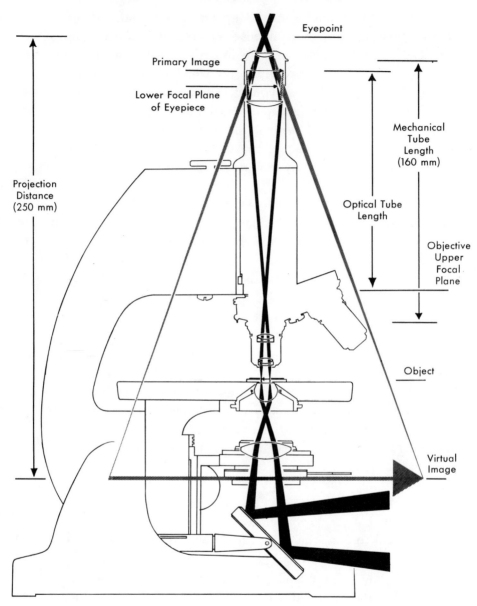

The path of light through a light microscope. *(Courtesy Bausch and Lomb Optical Company, Rochester, N.Y.)*

You may have noticed a few other differences between the way a microscope is used and the way a telescope is used. When you change the magnification power of a microscope, you change the objective. Telescope magnification is changed by changing the eyepiece. You can change the eyepiece on a microscope, too. For example, if you were using a 10× objective and a 10× eyepiece, the magnification would be 100×. If you changed the eyepiece to a 15× eyepiece, the magnification would be 150×. You could possibly change the object lens on a telescope, too, but that would be a much more difficult thing to do than just swinging around a new objective as is the case with a microscope.

Higher-priced, research-quality microscopes are likely to have at least one "oil immersion" objective. Oil-immersion objectives are used for high magnifications. To use an oil-immersion lens, a drop of clear, colorless oil is placed on a thin piece of glass or plastic called a cover glass or cover slip which is in place over the specimen so that the specimen is "sandwiched" between the cover slip and the slide. The cover slip keeps the oil away from the specimen. The objective is carefully lowered so that the tip is immersed in the oil. Why would anyone want to do that? At very high magnifications, a great deal of light is lost as it passes through the specimen—the air between the slide—and the objective and the lenses in the objective. The oil is of the same consistency as the glass of the lenses. By putting the oil on the slide, you eliminate the refraction or "rebending" of the light between the slide and the object. This saves light and gives a clearer, brighter image. The oil-immersion objective was perfected in 1878 by a famous German microscope maker, Ernst Abbe. He also invented the condenser.

The image produced by a microscope is similar to that produced by a telescope in many ways. The microscope image is upside down and "backwards." If you move the slide to the left, the image will seem to move to the right. If you move the slide up (away from you on this microscope), the image will appear to

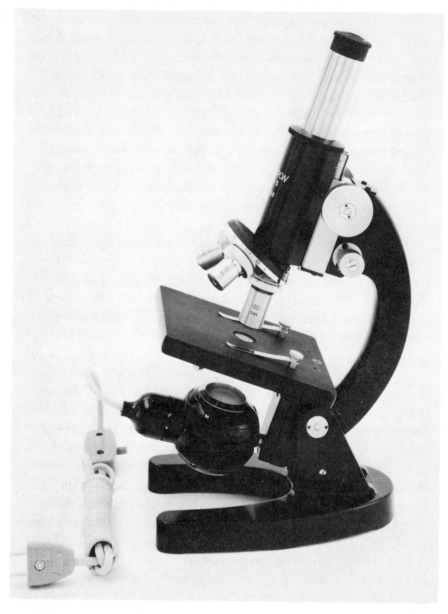

This type of microscope is widely used in high school and college science courses. Note the built-in light source and the iris diaphragm. *(Courtesy Unitron Instruments Inc.)*

move down. It seems strange, when you start to use a microscope, but you get used to it in a very short time.

We have been talking about **monocular microscopes.** Those are the ones with one eyepiece. There are also **binocular microscopes.** They have two eyepieces. Practically all microscopes used by scientists are binocular. Binoculars are much more comfortable to use than monocular microscopes. And, as you might expect, binocular microscopes usually cost much more than monocular microscopes.

Microscopes can be put together in a number of ways to fit a particular use. The microscope shown in the photo is an **inverted** mieroscope. Inverted is just a fancy way to say upside down. This kind of microscope is used to examine specimens that can't easily be put on slides. You can also examine specimens in certain kinds of glass containers without taking the specimens out of the container. For example, living cells can be kept alive through a method called *cell culture.* The cells are grown in flat round dishes. The cells tend to grow along the bottom of the dish. The objectives of an inverted microscope can be brought up to the bottom of the dish so that the cells can be examined without taking them out of the dish.

Microscopes can be equipped with still cameras and movie cameras. They can be hooked up to television monitors so that a roomful of people can look at a specimen at the same time. Some teaching microscopes are equipped with an extra eyepiece that sticks out from the body of the instrument. This arrangement allows the teacher and student to view a specimen at the same time without getting so close that they will bump heads. Other types of microscopes project the image like a film projector.

Preparing the specimens is a very important part of working with microscopes. You can't just throw something on a slide and expect to find out an awful lot about it. For most microscopes, the specimens have to be very thin. Some kinds of specimens, such as liquids, are already thin enough. Suppose, however, you wanted to examine something like the stem of a plant. If you put

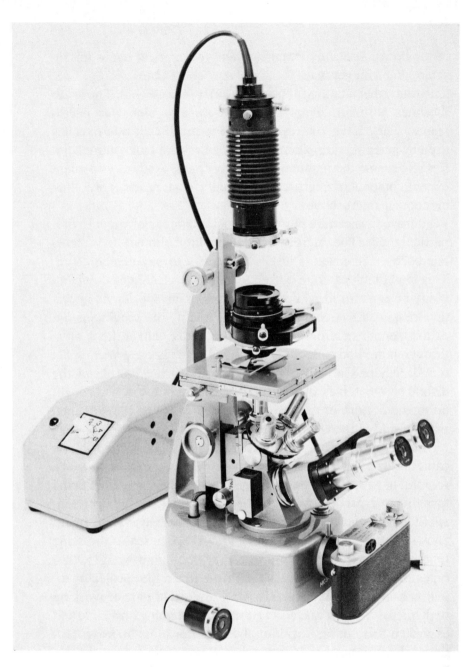

Inverted binocular microscopes such as this one are particularly useful for studying cell cultures. It is equipped for phase contrast. Note the camera at the base. *(Courtesy Unitron Instruments Inc.)*

a chunk of the stem on the slide and placed it under your microscope, you would see a black blob. In order to see anything in that stem, it will have to be cut into thin slices. Just how thick a slice depends on what you want to see, but a slice about fifty microns thick is typical. Compared to an ordinary potato chip, fifty microns is quite thin. You will remember that a micron is 1/1,000 of a millimeter, so fifty microns comes out to a twentieth of a millimeter, or, in the English system, about 1/1,250 of an inch.

If cutting a slice about fifty microns thick sounds difficult, that is because it *is* difficult. That is, it would be difficult to cut such thin slices with ordinary cutting tools. There are machines designed to cut material into sections that are that thin and still thinner. These machines are called **microtomes.** Some microtomes can cut sections less than one micron thick.

Cutting the material into thin sections is usually not the only thing that has to be done if you expect to see anything worth looking at. Frequently the section has to be **stained.** That is, various dyes, chemicals, and other coloring agents are applied to the specimen. This staining is done to bring out certain features that you might want to see. For example, most cells have a central part called the **nucleus.** To see the nucleus clearly in most cells it is necessary to stain the cells. There are stains that will stain the nucleus and nothing else in the cell. Other stains can help you identify what you are looking at. Certain bacteria, for example, take up stain in a particular way. Often the way the stain is taken up is the only way to tell one kind of bacteria from another.

Staining is a very useful technique. Over the past 150 or so years it has been developed into a fine art. Staining does have its disadvantages. In most instances, living material is killed if it is stained. There are many times, however, when scientists want to observe living material, and they want to observe that material in sharp detail. The cell culture mentioned earlier is an example. The scientist who is growing the cells certainly wants to see what is going on in those cells. If they are stained, however, the cells will usually be killed.

To meet the need for examining living material in detail, a kind of microscope called the **phase-contrast microscope** was developed. Light that passes through something as transparent as a layer of cells only a few microns thick does not give us much information about the cells. It is almost as though the light passed through plain glass. We see the glass, yet we don't see it. The phase-contrast microscope is designed to slow down and change the path of light through the microscope in a way that provides more contrast in the image. With a phase-contrast microscope it is possible to see details of the specimen without staining. The phase-contrast microscope is a very important instrument for biologists, those scientists who study living things.

Reflecting Microscopes

Yes, there are reflecting microscopes. They are not as widely used as reflecting telescopes. They are very expensive and are used in special applications where there must be absolutely no chromatic aberration. The objective is made up of a convex mirror and a concave mirror. The distance between the objective and the specimen can be much greater than it is with most microscopes. This characteristic makes the microscope useful for examining metals that are being heated in furnaces.

Dissecting Microscopes

These microscopes are sometimes called "stereo microscopes." They don't play rock music as you look into them, but they do produce a three-dimensional image. These microscopes feature low magnifications with very wide fields of view. As you might expect, dissecting microscopes are very useful for dissecting plant and animal specimens. They are also widely used for examining rocks, jewelry, and just about anything else, when

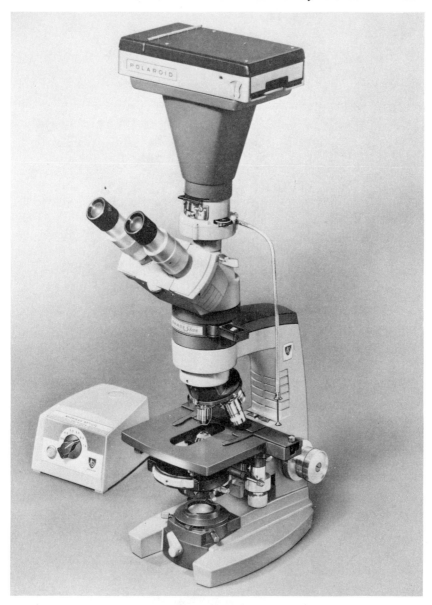

This microscope has a binocular eyepiece, phase contrast, and provision for photography. *(Courtesy American Optical Company, Buffalo, N.Y.)*

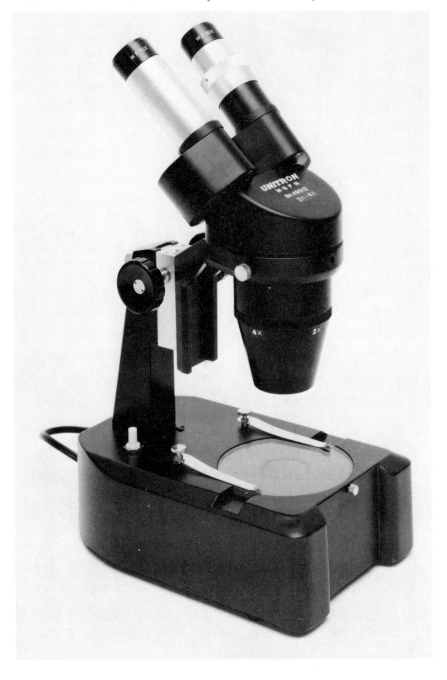

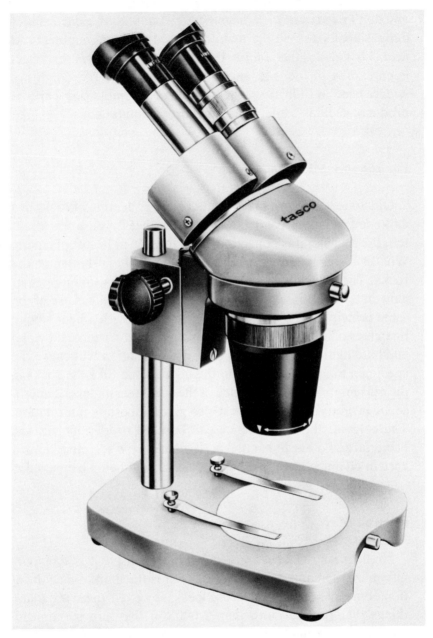

Two dissecting microscopes. The magnification is changed by rotating the cone-shaped lens housing. *(Courtesy Unitron Instruments Inc., and Tasco Sales, Inc., Miami, Fla.)*

you don't need very high magnification but require a clear three-dimensional view. These microscopes also have great **depth of field.** That means that a fairly thick section of a transparent specimen can be in focus at one time. Dissecting microscopes are widely used in industry to help workers assemble tiny parts of products such as cameras and electronic equipment.

Fluorescence Microscopes

Did you ever go to a museum that has a collection of rocks in a darkened room? If you have, you know that if you press a button, the rocks in this collection seem to glow in beautiful colors. What is happening there is that ultraviolet light is shining on the rocks. The ultraviolet radiation causes the rocks to **fluoresce** or glow in the dark. The fluorescence microscope makes use of the same principle. The microscope is equipped with a light source that gives off ultraviolet radiation (which we can't see) and violet and blue light (which we can see). This radiation will cause the specimen to appear to glow in the microscope (like the rocks in the museum). The fluorescence of the specimen under the microscope is pretty to look at, but it also gives important information. The color of the fluorescence can be used to identify viruses, bacteria, and other living things. It also lets the scientist know if certain chemicals are present in the material being examined.

Electron Microscopes

No light microscope, no matter how expensive it is, can magnify more than about 2,000 times. That is the limit of magnification obtained with light microscopes. However, there are many things that require more than 2,000× if they are to be seen. Viruses, for example, are much too small to be seen with light microscopes.

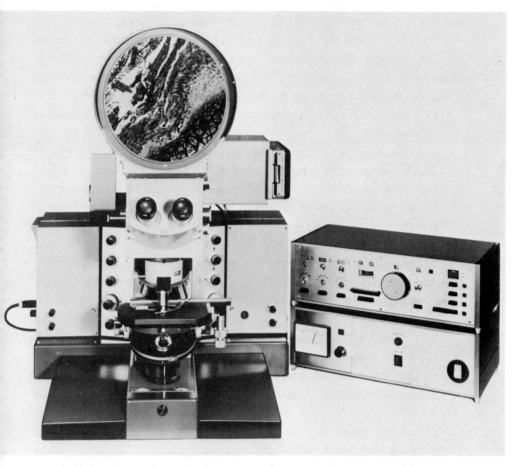

This lavishly equipped research microscope features photographic equipment and a projection device. *(Courtesy American Optical Company, Buffalo, N.Y.)*

Electron microscopes can achieve much higher magnifications than light microscopes. Magnifications of 100,000× and more are possible. Electron microscopes also have very high resolving power. Some can achieve resolutions as high as ten Angstroms. That means, the electron microscope can distinguish between two points only ten Angstroms apart (an Angstrom is 1/10,000 of a micron).

In an electron microscope a stream of electrons is used in much the same way that light is used in a light microscope. Electrons are one of the parts of an atom. A flow of electrons is electricity, and patterns of electrons on your television tube produce the picture.

The stream of electrons is bent, or refracted, by magnets that act as lenses. The electron stream passes through the specimen and through magnetic objectives. The electrons are projected by a magnetic projector lens (which corresponds to the eyepiece on a light microscope) onto a screen or onto photographic film. The electrons form an image of the specimen on the screen in much the same way a picture is formed on a television set.

The first electron microscopes were **transmission electron microscopes.** These are similar to light microscopes in the way that electrons pass through the specimen. Specimens for electron microscopes must be very thin, much thinner than specimens prepared for work with light microscopes.

Many important discoveries have been made with electron microscopes. Details of the way living cells are made were discovered with electron microscopes. They enabled scientists to see parts of cells that were not known to exist before electron microscopes were used. Other parts that could just be made out with light microscopes were seen more clearly. Viruses were seen for the first time.

There are some disadvantages to electron microscopes. Air must be pumped out of the path through which the electron stream travels. The air would scatter the electrons before they could pass through the specimen to produce a picture. Since the

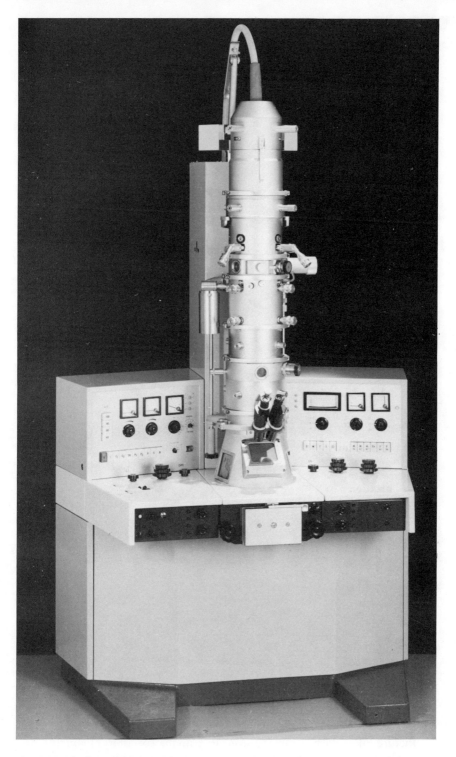

A transmission electron microscope. *(Courtesy Siemens Company)*

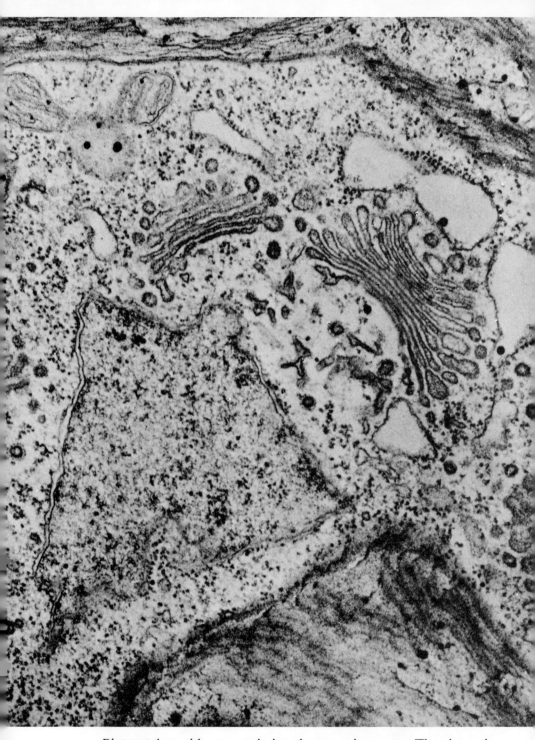

Picture taken with a transmission electron microscope. The picture is a micrograph of part of a cell from the pancreas of a guinea pig. The magnification is 50,000×. *(Courtesy Dr. George Palade and Dr. Keith Porter from the* CELL, *Upjohn Company)*

air must be pumped out to produce a vacuum, living material cannot usually be examined with an electron microscope. Electron microscopes produce images only in black and white.

Another kind of electron microscope is the **scanning electron microscope.** In a scanning electron microscope, the electrons do not pass through the specimen. The magnetic lenses of the scanning electron microscope focus the electrons into a tiny, bright spot. This spot of electrons scans the surface of the specimen. As the electrons strike the specimen surface, other types of radiation are "kicked out" of the surface. These radiations are picked up by a device similar to a television camera. This device converts the radiations to electrical signals which are sent to a computer. The computer analyzes the signals and produces an image of the specimen on a television monitor. Photographs of the image can be taken with built-in cameras.

The scanning electron microscope produces spectacular, breathtaking images that have a three-dimensional quality. Scanning electron microscopes can be useful at lower magnifications than transmission electron microscopes. Entire live insects, for example, can be examined with a scanning electron microscope. These microscopes have been useful in industry, producing detailed pictures of items such as tiny transistors and microscopically sized computer circuits.

Other types of electron microscopes have been used in recent years to produce images of single atoms. The electron microscopes that produced images of atoms were instruments that combined the features of scanning, transmission, and other types of electron microscopes.

Chances are that you won't buy an electron microscope to use around the house. Nor are you likely to invest several million dollars in a radio telescope. Of course, you might decide to become a scientist, in which case you might use instruments of that kind. For now, however, there are many types of telescopes and microscopes you can buy or make and you don't need a million dollars to own them.

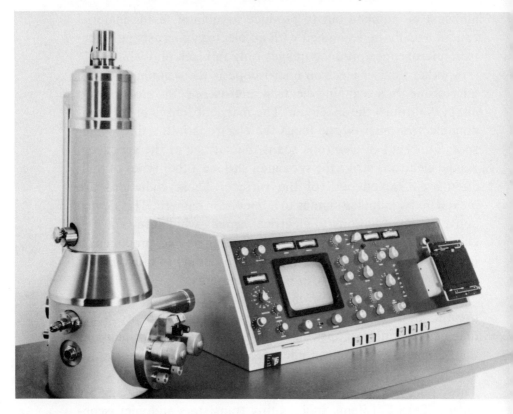

A scanning electron microscope. The image appears on the TV monitor. *(Courtesy AMR Corporation)*

Picture of the eye of a fruit fly taken with a scanning electron micro-scope. The magnification is 300×. *(Japan Electron Optics Limited [JEOL]).*

So You Want to Buy
a Microscope or Telescope

Buying a microscope or telescope is like buying anything else in most ways. You must shop carefully, comparing different makes of instruments with others to determine what is the best buy for your money. Like anything else, there are good, high-quality microscopes and telescopes, and there are some that are not so good. Practically anything can be made a little cheaper and flimsier so that it can be sold for less money. That tactic may make money for the company that sells the item, but it probably won't give a great deal of satisfaction to the buyer.

There are some important differences between microscopes, telescopes, and other things you can buy. A microscope or telescope can be a lifetime thing. With reasonable care they can last indefinitely; there is little on them that can wear out. The author has a microscope that is over fifty years old. It is no less useful today than when it was first made. Once you buy a good telescope or microscope, the only reason for ever parting with it is to "graduate" to a bigger one or to trade it in for a better one. The longer you keep your microscope or telescope and, more important, the more you use it, the more pleasure you will get from it.

How much will you have to pay for a good microscope or telescope? Questions about cost are always the most difficult to answer. Prices vary widely, depending on quality, features, and the use to which the instrument will be put. For example, one of the expenses a medical student has to bear is the cost of a microscope. The student will use this instrument not only in his or her studies in medical school but also after graduation. For the medical student to buy a cheap, low-quality instrument is throwing money away. The student will put that microscope to hard, daily use. A medical student would be much better off with a binocular microscope because more work can be done with much less eye strain. The student can expect to spend at least $2,000 for a microscope of acceptable quality. A hobbyist does not need to spend near that amount of money for a microscope. Of course you can, if you want to and have the money, but it's really not necessary.

Although microscopes and telescopes do not have to cost a fortune, they do cost more than most toys, games, athletic equipment or almost anything else you might buy to play with or to pursue a hobby. On the other hand, you can expect a microscope or telescope to last much, much longer than any toy. In general, telescopes or microscopes suitable for serious use by an amateur run to about the same money as good, single-lens reflex cameras. What does that mean in dollars? In 1980, you could buy a good, perfectly acceptable three-inch refractor for around $300 to $500. You could pay a little less and still get a good instrument. On the other hand, you could pay a little more and not get much more in quality. You could buy a very good monocular microscope for about the same money. There are also many fine microscopes available for less than $200, but not much less. That may sound like an awful lot of money — $200, $500 — and it is, for most of us. If you stop to think about it, a good ten-speed bike can cost about that much. Although a bicycle should last a long time if you take care of it, it will not give you a fraction of the years of service you can expect from a good microscope or telescope.

Think again about all that stuff you got for birthdays over the years. How much of it do you still use? How much of it is in an attic or basement or sold off in a tag sale so it can sit in somebody else's attic? The total cost of all that stuff could well have been the cost of a good microscope or telescope. A good-quality

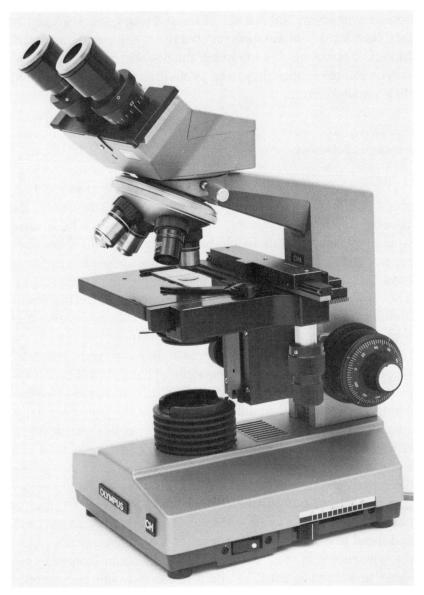

A research-quality binocular microscope. *(Courtesy Olympus Corporation of America, New Hyde Park, N.Y.)*

optical instrument will last for years and years, much longer, in fact, than most automobiles that cost twenty-five times as much. In fact, it is not at all uncommon for people to give the microscopes and telescopes they used as children to their children and their grandchildren.

Buying a Telescope

Depending on where you live, finding where to buy a telescope can be a problem. If you live in a small town or in the country, far from a big city, there probably won't be a store where you can just walk in and buy a telescope. Fine telescopes are not as widely sold in stores as are most other items. Some department and discount stores may carry a line of telescopes. They are usually sold in the camera department. In other stores they may be kept in a hobby department. You might also find them in some camera stores and optical shops.

Although interest in amateur astronomy is growing, telescopes are still not a high-volume item. (That is, a store can't expect them to sell as fast as television sets or stereos, for example.) Because they do not move as fast as the consumer items advertised on television, a store manager is not likely to devote a lot of selling space for them. There is only so much space in a store, and the store manager must give most of the space to the items that sell fast and in high volume. For that reason, the selection of telescopes and microscopes in a department store is likely to be limited at best, although there are a few stores here and there that have excellent lines of these instruments. Also, the salespeople in most department and discount stores are not likely to know a great deal about telescopes and microscopes even if they do sell them.

Telescopes can be bought by mail order, and if you live far from a big city that might be the only way. There are many fine, reputable companies that sell telescopes by mail. Of course,

A 3-inch refractor. This instrument has a focal length of 1,200 mm. (*Courtesy Tasco Sales*)

buying by mail order has its own set of problems. You really don't know what you're getting until the item you ordered is delivered. Few, if any, of the companies that sell telescopes will deliberately try to cheat you, but a bad telescope could be shipped out by accident, for example. If something is wrong with the telescope you buy, or if you are not satisfied with its performance, you can return it. However, returning things by mail is a bother and a hassle. You have to pack it for shipment and then wait weeks or months to get another one or have the one you bought fixed. So, if at all possible, buy your telescope from a dealer. You can try it out before you buy, and the dealer is right there to set things right if there are any problems.

A good way to find out where to buy a telescope is to ask an amateur astronomer. There might be a few around where you live. If not, go to the library and get a copy of a magazine called *Sky and Telescope.* You will find many advertisements from telescope companies. Copy down the names and addresses of these companies and write to them for a catalogue. Some companies might ask for a dollar or two for the catalogue.

Just looking through a magazine like *Sky and Telescope* can give you a pretty good idea of the many different kinds of telescopes you can buy and what they cost. You should check several issues of the magazine. Not all the companies advertise in every issue. There is a section in the back where people advertise used telescopes for sale. You might pick up a real bargain in a used telescope. On the other hand, you could get stuck with a piece of junk. On the average, used telescopes are much less likely to be "lemons" than are used cars. But before you buy a used telescope, you should arrange to try it first.

The first decision you will have to make is whether you want a refractor or a reflector. That is not an easy decision to make. Both types have their good and bad points. Some of these points are outlined in the table below. The comparisons are between refractors and Newtonian reflectors. The other kinds of reflectors have their own good and bad points.

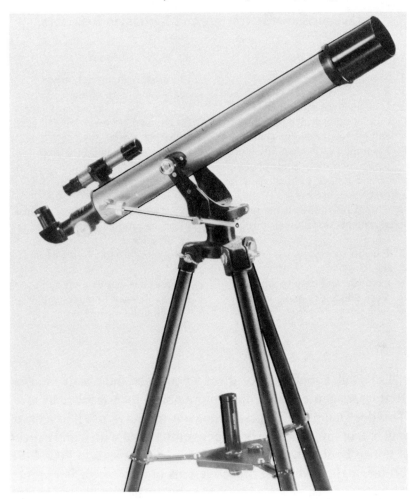

A 2.4-inch refractor on an altazimuth mounting. The instrument has a focal length of 710 mm. *(Courtesy Tasco Sales)*

A Comparison of Refractors and Newtonian Reflectors.

Refractors	*Newtonian Reflectors*
1. More rugged	More easily disturbed; needs adjustment more often
2. Usually costs more than reflectors for comparable resolving and light-gathering power	Usually costs less than refractors for comparable resolving and light-gathering power
3. Even the best have a little chromatic aberration; some cheap ones can have so much as to be practically useless	No chromatic aberration from the mirror; best for color photography
4. Closed tube protects internal parts; cuts down on air turbulence	Open tube can allow dirt and dust to get on internal parts; increases air turbulence
5. Easy to set up and use; no waiting	A bit more trouble to set up and use
6. Compact and easy to store	Larger ones can be a bit bulky
7. Very difficult to make yourself	Relatively easy to make yourself— including the mirror!

Let's talk about some of these advantages and disadvantages. Refractors can certainly take more abuse than most reflectors. This does not mean you can drop your refractor, use it as a baseball bat, or hit your little brother over the head with it and expect it not to be damaged (not to mention the damage to your little brother). However, the objective lens of a refractor is put into place to stay where it is supposed to be. Little knocks and bumps are not likely to harm it too much. Of course, the object glass can't be put in just any old way. It has to be placed "square" in the tube. That, however, is done at the factory, and once the objective is there it tends to stay if you treat the telescope with any amount of respect. You might have to make some slight adjustment when you first get it. Instructions for doing so are in the owner's manual that comes with the instrument.

Both mirrors of a reflector must be in exact alignment with each other if you expect to get a good image. While this align-

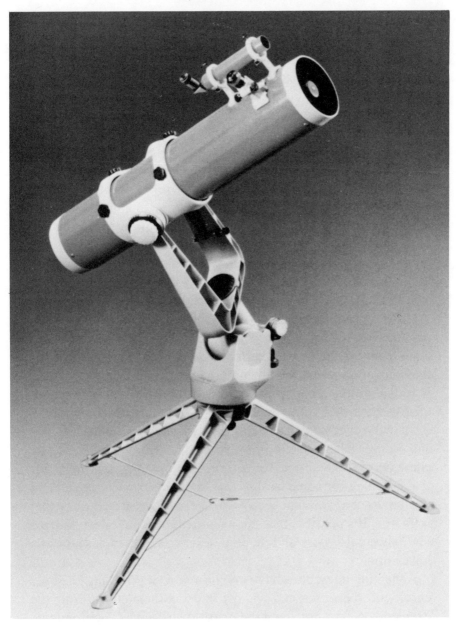

A 6-inch reflector on a yoke-type equatorial mounting. *(Courtesy Edmund Scientific Company, Barrington, N.J.)*

ment also may be done at the factory, the mirrors tend to get out of alignment in shipping. They also tend to get out of alignment whenever the telescope is moved from one place to another. The instruction book you get with your reflector will not only give you instructions for aligning the mirrors, it will tell you that there is an almost 100 percent chance that you will have to do so before you can use the telescope.

Adjusting the mirrors of a reflector is not a difficult thing to do, once you have learned how to do it. You probably won't have to adjust the mirrors *every* time you use the telescope, but you will adjust them more often than you would have to adjust the lenses of a refractor. Adjusting screws for the main mirror are at the back of the tube. There are usually three of these. There are many different kinds of ways to place the secondary mirror in the telescope. For most of these, you will have to reach just inside the tube to make the necessary adjustments.

Good refractors generally cost more than reflectors. When dealing with smaller telescopes, a reflector mirror is more or less equivalent for light-gathering and resolving power to an objective lens of about half its diameter. Therefore, a six-inch mirror is roughly equivalent to a three-inch objective glass. A good-quality three-inch refracting telescope generally costs more than a six-inch reflector equal in other ways, such as mounting. This situation can be a useful point when you are shopping. If you come across a three-inch or a three-and-one-half-inch refractor that is selling for considerably less than most six-inch reflectors you have seen, you had better find out why before you buy that refractor. It's possible that the manufacturer could have taken a few "shortcuts" here and there in order to sell the telescope at a lower price.

Reflecting telescopes have no chromatic aberration. The only chromatic aberration you will get in using them comes from the eyepiece. Refractors, even the ones advertised as "achromatic" and "with coated lenses," will give you some chromatic aberration. In fact, too much chromatic aberration is the major prob-

A 4¼-inch reflector. A relatively inexpensive instrument such as this one is a first telescope for many hobbyists. *(Courtesy Edmund Scientific Company, Barrington, N.J.)*

lem of low-cost refractors. The chromatic aberration of the refractor is seen as a bluish tinge or haze around the object under observation. It is most noticeable when viewing bright objects such as the Moon and Venus. It is particularly bothersome if you want to do some color photography with your telescope. Reflectors are by far the best telescopes to use for taking color photographs of sky objects. That bargain-priced refractor we spoke of a little bit earlier—the one that cost less than most six-inch reflectors—could be equipped with low-quality lenses that will produce enough chromatic aberration to drive you up the wall.

The open-tube design of the reflector does present a few problems. The major problem in the reflector tube design is air currents in the tube. During the day when the telescope is sitting around the house, it warms up. At night, when you take it out, it cools down. The air inside the tube also cools down. This cooling sets up air currents in the tube. As the temperatures of the surrounding air and the tube and air in the tube equalize, the currents slow down and stop. While this turbulence is going on, it interferes with image formation.

You get some of this air movement in refractors, too, but not nearly as much. You might have to wait a while on some nights before you can use your reflector, but much of the time will be spent in setting up, so you won't notice it too much. This advantage of the refractor over the reflector is apparent. The refractor is certainly easier to set up.

The air-turbulence problem is seen mostly on reflectors that have metal tubes. Metals are good conductors of heat. Many telescope manufacturers offer reflectors that have tubes made of poor heat conductors such as plastics. Plastics, however, tend to have more "give" than metal, and you may have to adjust the mirror in a plastic tube more often.

You might have a bit of a problem finding a good place to store your reflector. A six-inch reflector, for example, requires a tube that is at least seven inches in diameter and, depending on the focal length, the tubes can be quite long.

An 8-inch reflector on an equatorial mounting. This telescope has a focal length of 2,500 mm. *(Courtesy Edmund Scientific Company, Barrington, N.J.)*

The last item in the list comparing refractors and Newtonian reflectors might lead you to say, "What! Me make a telescope?" You certainly could make a telescope. Thousands of people have made their own telescopes — reflecting telescopes, that is — and so can you.

"Folded Optics" Reflectors

Interest in amateur astronomy has grown quickly in the past twenty years or so. More people are buying telescopes than ever before, and more of the buyers are turning to Cassegrain and Maksutov reflectors.

One reason for the growing interest in these telescopes is the very effective promotion and advertising and selling ability of the two leading manufacturers of these instruments. Another reason is the convenience of the instruments. These instruments give the user long focal lengths in "folded" packages. They present many of the advantages of reflectors, such as hardly any chromatic aberration, and they have few of the disadvantages of Newtonian reflectors — bulkiness, open tube, need for frequent adjustment of mirror.

Folded-optics telescopes are extremely compact and easy to move. This characteristic has made them popular with city apartment dwellers. The telescopes can be put into the car and driven out to the country where there are no distracting city lights. Of course, you can do the same with most refractors, but a Cassegrain with a focal length of eighty inches could be easily put in the front seat of the smallest compact car. It would be difficult to get a refractor of similar focal length into the front seat of such a car, and for most Newtonian reflectors of the same focal length it would be impossible.

There are other advantages to these telescopes. The short tubes present less surface to the wind, and they are less likely to shake and shudder when the wind blows. The short tube also

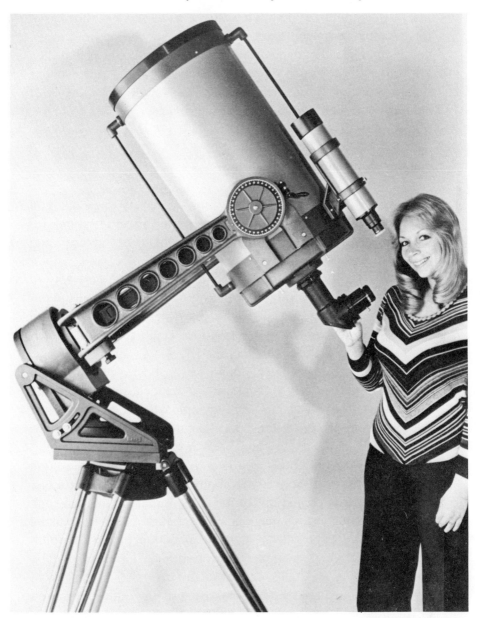

A 14-inch Cassegrain reflector on an equatorial mounting. This instrument provides a focal length of 3,900 mm that can be utilized for an effective highest magnification of about 840×. *(Courtesy Celestron International)*

means the mountings do not have to be as massive as those used for Newtonian reflectors.

The main disadvantage of folded optics telescopes is that they are rather expensive. You pay much more for these telescopes than you would for a refractor or for a Newtonian reflector of similar resolution and light-gathering power.

Judging the Quality of a Telescope

There are three main things to look for in any telescope you are checking out: (1) quality of lenses and mirrors (optics), (2) mechanics (focusing mechanisms, tube quality, et cetera), and (3) the mounting.

Optical quality is the most difficult to judge. The only way to really find out how good the optics are is to use the instrument. There are, however, certain things that can at least give you an idea of how one particular telescope might stack up against others as far as optics are concerned.

First of all, be very suspicious of exaggerated magnification claims. Be particularly suspicious if magnification is about the only thing in the sales pitch. Many people who are first buyers of telescopes are likely to think that magnification is the most important thing about a telescope. Well, it *is* something to consider, but it is not the only thing you need to know about a telescope before you buy it. Practically anybody who wants to make a fast buck can put some lenses in a tube and put them in there in such a way that will give high magnifications, but that does not make a good telescope. You will get high magnification, but, in all probability, you will get a magnified view of nothing. The image will be blurred, lacking in detail, and practically useless. The image will be so dim you will hardly be able to see it. The tiniest vibration of the tube will be magnified; the image will dance as though it were at a disco. At high magnifications, the field of view is very narrow, as well. You would be better off looking at the object with your unaided eye.

A 4¼-inch reflector on an equatorial mounting. *(Courtesy Edmund Scientific Company)*

The only magnification that is worth anything is *meaningful* magnification, which is just another way of saying clear, sharp images that tell you something about what you are looking at. Experienced amateur astronomers hardly ever use their highest powers. Most useful observations are made at the medium to lower powers. With lower powers you get wider fields of view and brighter images. The higher-power magnifications provide meaningful magnification only under the best conditions. Remember that when you look at a planet or star with your telescope, you are looking through the atmosphere. The atmosphere is not going to remain politely quiet, calm, and crystal clear just for you. The atmosphere is a swirling, seething mass of turbulence. This turbulence is also magnified by the telescope. Just how much the atmosphere interferes with observations is a matter of weather and how close to the horizon your observations are. The closer to the horizon, the more atmosphere you are looking through and the more turbulence you are likely to get. At high powers, the turbulence could make what you are looking at seem to be swimming in thick, steaming soup.

The meaningful magnification obtainable with a telescope is a matter of the focal length of the objective lens and the quality of that lens. It is also a matter of the *aperture* of the lens, or the width of the lens. The larger the aperture, the more meaningful the magnification you are likely to get, depending on lens quality.

The magnification of a telescope is found by dividing the focal length of the object lens by the focal length of the eyepiece. (When you do this division, be sure all the measurements are in the same system. Both metric and English systems are used.) Suppose, for example, you know that your telescope has a focal length of sixty inches. You want to find out what the magnification is when you use an eyepiece with a focal length of 4 mm. If you divide the 60 by 4, you will get an answer of 15×. That doesn't sound like much and it isn't; you have mixed up your units. Expressed in the metric system, the focal length of that telescope is 1,500 mm. The highest-power eyepiece usually supplied with a telescope is a 4-mm eyepiece. So, theoretically, the highest power of a telescope with a focal length of 1,500 mm is about $375 \times (1500 \div 4 = 375)$. But that eyepiece can be used only in the best possible conditions. Most of the time, you won't be too happy with what you see with the 4-mm eyepiece. A 6-mm eyepiece would give you 250×, and a 12-mm eyepiece would give you 125×. Most of the time, meaningful magnification will be limited to what you get with a 6-mm or 9-mm eyepiece, but even then conditions have to be good. A general rule you can follow is that meaningful magnification is limited to 50× to 60× per inch of mirror diameter with a reflector and about 75× per inch of aperture with a refractor.

You might see an ad for a small telescope, say a 2.4-inch refractor, either in a magazine or store display that includes claims such as, "300×! See the rings of Saturn!" How do advertisers get away with those kinds of claims? They get away with it through the use of a type of lens called a *Barlow lens*. With this lens, the magnification obtained with any particular eyepiece can be doubled or even tripled. The Barlow lens, when fitted to the eyepiece, changes the path of the light to give a greatly magnified image. So, if the manufacturer supplies a Barlow lens with the telescope, he has some justification, although a very weak one, for claiming those high magnifications. What they might not tell you is that the Barlow narrowly restricts the field of view, produces a very dim image, and multiplies the bad effects of vibration and air turbulence. A Barlow lens is not a bad thing to have. When viewing conditions are at their absolute best, a Barlow lens can enable you to study details of the moon's surface and the surface of a planet with a small telescope. But remember, there are very few nights in the year that will give you those kinds of conditions.

Another thing to consider is the *focal ratio*. The focal ratio is obtained by dividing the focal length of the lens or mirror by the aperture. For example, an eight-inch reflector with a focal length of 40 inches would have a focal ratio of 5, expressed as "f/5."

A 3-inch reflector on an altazimuth mounting with slow-motion controls. The inset shows eyepieces and a dust cover. *(Courtesy Tasco Sales)*

The smaller the focal ratio a telescope of a particular aperture has, the shorter the tube length is likely to be. Small focal ratios also give a wider field of view and better image brightness. The smaller the focal ratio, the better the telescope is likely to be for photography. Small focal-ratio telescopes are referred to as "fast" telescopes. Longer focal-ratio instruments are likely to give higher magnifications for a given aperture but the images will be dimmer, and a little arithmetic will tell you that the larger the focal ratio, the longer the telescope is likely to be. Reflectors generally have focal ratios between f/5 and f/8, although some, particularly Cassegrain types, will have f/10 and even f/11. Refractors tend to have focal ratios between f/12 and f/20. Most small refractors intended for amateur use are around f/15. Generally, the lower focal ratios of small reflectors tend to uphold the opinion that they are better for photography than are small refractors.

The resolving power of a telescope is all important, and, if any one quality of a telescope is more important than another, resolving power is more important than magnification. As mentioned earlier, resolving power is determined by the aperture and quality of the object glass or mirror.

Some object glasses will give you better resolution than others, but there is a limit beyond which even the best cannot go. This is the *Dawes limit,* named after the English astronomer William R. Dawes (1799–1868). This limit is obtained by dividing 4.56 by the aperture of the telescope in inches. The result is a value that is read as *seconds of an arc.* So the *theoretical* limit of a three-inch object glass would be 1.52 seconds of an arc, which means that the object glass can "separate" two stars that close together into two points of light.

The word "theoretical" is the catch. Just because 4.56 divided by 3 equals 1.52 does not mean that every three-inch object glass will give you that resolution. There is quality of lenses to consider and even the best of these is at the mercy of the weather. The only way to check out the resolution claims of the manufacturer is to use the telescope. However, if the sales pitch (printed or spoken) does not even mention resolution in terms of seconds of an arc, you might begin to think that the resolving power of that telescope being peddled is not something to brag about.

The quality of the object glass is all important. The lenses must be *achromatic* if they are to be of much use. Though achromatic means "without color," that does not mean you will have no color at all. What achromatic really means in connection with a refracting telescope is that the object glass has been color corrected. Color correction is important and adds to the price of the telescope, but it is definitely worth the extra cost. Chances are that if the manufacturer does not say the object glass is achromatic, it is not.

The lens should be coated. The coating gives a bluish-purplish cast to the lens and it helps to improve the image. However, the claim "fully coated" lenses does not necessarily mean that the object glass is achromatic. All better-quality lenses are both coated and achromatic.

Better-quality object glasses are air spaced. That means there is a space of air between the lenses. Again, these are more expensive than those object glasses that are not air spaced. So, if you're interested in a refractor, be sure to ask if the object glasses are achromatic and air spaced. In cheaper object glasses, the lenses are glued together with a transparent cement. There is nothing really wrong with doing that; however, object glasses with cemented lenses will not usually give you as good an image as object glasses with air-spaced lenses.

The choice of eyepieces is also important. When you first buy your telescope, there is usually no choice—you must take what the manufacturer supplies. However, you can buy all kinds of eyepieces later. As mentioned before, shorter focal-length eyepieces give higher magnification than those of longer focal length. But the greater the magnification, the narrower the field of view and the dimmer the image. Another thing to consider

This neat little Maksutov reflector is equipped with a diagonal-prism eyepiece. It has a 1,000-mm focal length and can be used as a telephoto lens for a camera. The Maksutov shell is visible at the front of the instrument. *(Courtesy Celestron International)*

about eyepieces is *eye relief.* Eye relief is how close you have to hold your eye to the eyepiece. Holding your eye right down to the eyepiece gets uncomfortable after a while. So, an eyepiece with a better eye relief, one that enables you to get a little space between your eye and the eyepiece, is desirable.

Following is a list of some of the more common types of eyepieces and some information about their good and bad points.

HUYGENIAN: One of the most widely used; commonly supplied with small, low-priced telescopes. Eye relief poor. Edge focus tends to be blurred. Price: low.

RAMSDEN: Commonly supplied with low-priced microscopes; edge focus better than Huygenian; color correction, poor, but *Kellner* variation provides much better color correction (achromatic Ramsden and Kellner not exactly the same, but similar); wide field of view; fair eye relief, but suffers from stray reflections that result in "ghosting"; dust and dirt on lenses more likely to be seen in image than with other types. Price: low.

ERFLE: Very wide field; good for deep-space, low-power viewing; ghosting rather bad. Price: expensive.

MONOCENTRIC: Designed to reduce ghosting; excellent for highpower work. Price: expensive.

ORTHROSCOPIC: Seldom supplied with low-priced telescopes, frequently supplied with better-quality instruments; wide field of view, good for low and medium magnifications; good eye relief, some ghosting but not as severe as Ramsden. Price: expensive.

TOLLES: An unusually constructed eyepiece, it is a single cylinder of glass rather than separate lenses; excellent color correction; good for use with reflectors; excellent for high-power work. Price: fairly expensive.

It would seem that no one type of eyepiece is the best for all the different kinds of observing you might care to do. As an amateur astronomer becomes more experienced, he or she will acquire more eyepieces. After a while, you learn which eyepieces are best to use in different situations. An eyepiece can make all the difference in telescope performance. You might be very disappointed with the performance you get with a 6-mm Huygenian supplied by the manufacturer, but put a 12.5-mm orthoscopic in there and you just might be pleasantly amazed (assuming the orthoscopic is of good quality). Most eyepieces have a 1 1/4-inch barrel. Some, used for extra-wide field work, have bigger barrels. They must be used with tube adapters.

Some refractors are equipped with a *star diagonal prism* at the end of the instrument. This arrangement of prisms allows for more comfortable viewing of objects high above the horizon. With a star diagonal prism you don't have to get down on your knees or lie on your back when the telescope is pointed up at a sharp angle. The disadvantage of using the star diagonal prism is that some light is lost as the light passes through the prism. Use it only when you absolutely have to.

Mirrors

When buying a reflector, you have to put a great deal of faith in the manufacturer. The only way to find out about the quality of the mirrors in the telescope is to use the telescope. However, there are certain things to look for that can give you an idea of the general quality of the instrument.

A fairly good indication of general quality is the way the secondary mirror is mounted. The cheap way is with a flat piece of metal attached to what amounts to a piece of thick, round wire. The wire sticks up through a hole in the tube and into the focusing mechanism. The flat piece of metal is at an angle, to pick up the light reflected from the main mirror. That kind of secondary mirror mount gets out of alignment if you so much as breathe on it; it requires constant adjustment. A better way to place the secondary mirror is in an adjustable cell secured to the inner walls of the telescope tube.

Carefully follow the manufacturer's instruction for adjusting the mirrors. If the telescope still gives poor results after you are *sure* both the main and the secondary mirror are adjusted, bring it back for advice or return it, if you are really unhappy with it.

Finder telescopes

' Every telescope intended for astronomical use, no matter how inexpensive, should be equipped with at least one *finder telescope*. The finder telescope is a small, low-power, wide-field-of-view refracting telescope attached to the tube of the main telescope. As the name suggests, it is used to locate the particular object you are interested in observing. It is not usually necessary to use the finder for observing the Moon, which is never a problem to find. For just about everything else, however (with the possible exception of Venus), you will need to use the finder.

To be useful, the finder should have an object glass at least 1 3/4 inches in diameter—two inches is better. Unfortunately, you are not likely to find a finder scope meeting those qualifications on most low-cost telescopes. Sometimes, if you come across a telescope that is a good buy in every respect except for an unusable finder, it may pay you to buy the instrument anyway and get a better finder scope later. Finders with diagonals are easier to use then those with straight eyepieces. With the latter, you sometimes have to twist your neck into contortions and press your face against the main telescope tube.

The finder scope should have adjustable focusing, preferably with rack-and-pinion mechanisms controlled with a knob. Some can't be focused, and others have slide or twist focusing arrangements that are difficult to control. The finder should have cross-

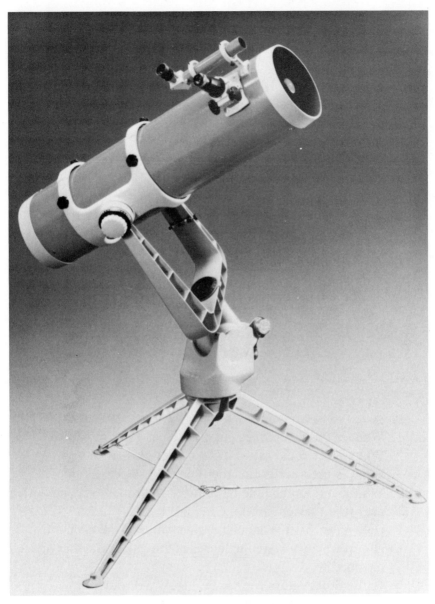

This 8-inch reflector has a diagonal eyepiece on the finder that makes it comfortable to use. *(Courtesy Edmund Scientific Company)*

hair marks inside, somewhat like those of a rifle scope. One of your first jobs with any telescope you buy, refractor or reflector, is *collimating* the finder and the main telescope. This is adjusting the finder so that what you see in it is exactly what you will see in the main telescope. It is obvious that if the finder is not properly collimated there is not much point in having it.

Optical-quality Summary

Following are the questions you should ask a salesperson before you buy a telescope. If he or she cannot answer the questions or claims that the question is unimportant, that salesperson does not know much about telescopes. This does not necessarily mean you should not buy the telescope from that person; you might be picking up a good buy. But you do have to remember that if you have any problem or need advice, the salesperson who doesn't know what you are talking about when you ask these questions will probably not be able to help you.

Questions to ask the Salesperson:
  1. What is the focal length of the object glass or mirror?
  2. What is the focal ratio of the object glass or mirror?
  3. What is the aperture of the object glass or mirror?
  4. What is the obtainable resolution in terms of seconds of an arc? (the Dawes limit)
  5. (For reflectors.) What is the wave value of the main mirror?
  6. (For refractors.) Are the lenses in the object glass air-spaced or glued?
  7. Is the object glass (refractors) truly achromatic?
  8. What kind of eyepieces are supplied?
  9. Can I bring it back within a reasonable time (find out how long) if I'm not too happy with it?

Mechanics

The tube of a refractor should be made out of sturdy metal, and the metal should be reasonably thick and painted a dull black on the inside. If the tube has a "tinny" feel when you tap it with your fingers, it is probably of inferior quality.

Make sure the tube of a refractor has a sufficient *dew cap*. The dew cap is the part of the tube that extends out over the object lens. Its purpose is to prevent, or at least cut down, the formation of dew on the object lens. The idea is for the dew to form on the cap and not on the object glass. The length of the dew cap should be about three times the diameter of the object glass. If it is less, you might have trouble, depending on conditions. The bothersome thing is that dew is most likely to be a problem on clear cool nights that are, in every other respect, best for working with your telescope.

Dewing is also a problem with reflectors. In time, too much dew forming on a mirror can damage the surface. Most of the dewing problems with reflectors are involved with the secondary mirror. Protection is offered by mounting the secondary as far in from the opening of the tube as possible.

Many inexpensive telescopes do not have long enough dew caps. To provide an effective dew cap, the manufacturer must use more material, and that adds to the cost of manufacturing. If the dew cap is too short, you can buy or make an extension. The extension is essentially an open cylinder or cone painted black on the inside. There can also be problems if the dew cap is too long. A too-long dew cap can cut down the aperture of the object glass.

The focusing mechanism should be of the rack-and-pinion type. There should be hardly any "give" or "play" in the control knob. When you turn the knob, the slide tube that moves in and out should move. If you can twist the knob back and forth and nothing happens, the focusing mechanism is not of very good quality. Also, once you move the tube to where you want it, it should stay there. It should not "creep" out of position.

Move the focusing mechanism back and forth. Does it move smoothly? It should not be too stiff or too loose. Does the telescope shake and quiver when you operate the focusing mechanism? Shaking and quivering is a sign of poor construction.

Mountings

The finest, most expensive telescope that money can buy is absolutely useless unless it is on a good mounting. There are two basic types of telescope mountings: the altazimuth and the equatorial. Both types of mountings are designed to help you cope with a situation that is not always obvious but is of vital importance to any user of astronomical telescopes, from the novice amateur to a Nobel Prize-winning radio astronomer. That situation concerns the movement of the "platform" from which you are making your observations. Your platform is the Earth and, as you well know, the Earth is not standing still. It is spinning on its axis and revolving around the sun. This movement may not always be obvious to you. If you look at a star, that star seems to be staying right where it is. But if you look through a telescope pointed at it, and that telescope has no provision for "tracking," the star will drift across your field of view and out of it in a very short time. Of course, the higher the magnification, the shorter will be that star's stay in your field of view.

Altazimuth Mountings

If you hold a telescope in your hands, it does not take you very long to figure out that there are two general directions in which you can move the telescope—up and down, back and

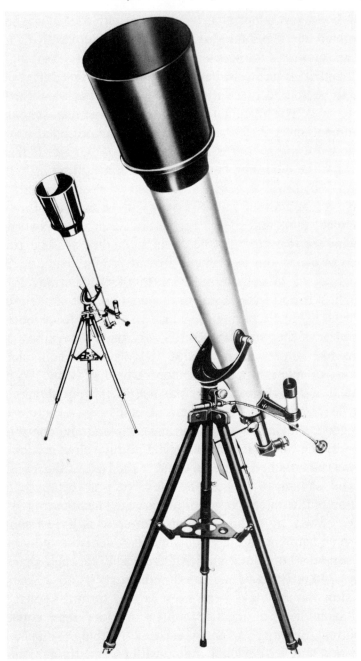

This 2-inch refractor is equipped with an altazimuth mounting and slow-motion controls. *(Courtesy Tasco Sales)*

forth. If you try to look at a star or planet with a telescope held in your hand, it will not take you very long to discover that a hand-held astronomical telescope is about the most useless thing ever put together. It has to be held firmly by something, but you also have to be able to move it up and down and back and forth (or side to side). The altazimuth mounting does just that. It holds the instrument and enables you to move it in a controlled way.

The word *altazimuth* is a combination of two words that tell you what the mounting does. The "alt" comes from *altitude,* or the up and down or height adjustment of the telescope; "azimuth" is just another way of saying side to side, or horizontal. You might think that all you need is something like a swivel bolt to swing the telescope up and down and a disk of some kind on which to swing the instrument around for the azimuth. Sadly enough, many manufacturers think that kind of arrangement is enough. It is not. In order to get the most use out of a telescope, you need to have accurate, *slow-motion* control. Remember that the image of that star or planet is very highly magnified. What seems like a very slight motion to you is the equivalent of millions of miles in your telescope's field of view. With the slightest nudge, that planet or star will seem to go flying out of your field of view to some other universe.

A good altazimuth mounting has slow-motion controls for both altitude and azimuth. A typical altitude slow-motion control is a rod attached to the tube and to the base of the mounting. The rod is clamped in when the telescope is at the approximate position of the object you want to look at. The telescope is then moved slowly by turning a knob. Better ones have knobs for coarse adjustment and fine adjustment. A separate rod controls the azimuth (horizontal motion), preferably through gears and rollers. Other types of altazimuth mountings do not have a rod. The slow-motion movements are made by turning knobs.

Altazimuth mountings generally cost less than equatorial mountings. So what's wrong with them? Nothing. You just have to work a little harder than you do with an equatorial mounting.

To keep the planet or star in your field of view, you have to constantly adjust both the altitude and the azimuth. It's a bit tricky, but you learn how with practice. The largest optical telescope in the world, the 236-inch reflector in the Soviet Union, is on an altazimuth mounting. Its movements, of course, are controlled by a computer, but that computer still has to be adjusted for both altitude and azimuth.

Equatorial Mountings

Are equatorial mountings worth the extra cost? The answer to that question is "yes" with a few "ifs." If you plan to do a lot of astrophotography, an equatorial mounting is a must. If you want to concentrate more on your observations and less on turning rods and knobs, then you should get an equatorial mounting. If you are really serious about your astronomy hobby, then the equatorial mounting is the one you should go for. A good equatorial mounting is costly, but if you are just the least bit handy with tools, you could make an equatorial mounting yourself. Other than its cost, the only other major disadvantage of the equatorial mounting is that it is a bit more difficult to understand than the altazimuth mounting.

As you probably know, the Earth is tilted on its axis. The first step in making an equatorial mounting is to tilt the telescope so that it is parallel to the tilt of the Earth. Another way of saying that is, tilt the telescope until it is pointing at the North Star, or tilt the telescope so that the angle formed by the telescope and the horizon is equal to the latitude of your location. That tilt is called the *polar axis.*

Of course you can't use your hands to hold the telescope at the polar axis. It has to be mounted on something that will hold it there. There are many ways of doing this, and one of the most widely used methods is the so-called *German mounting.*

The German mounting is in the shape of a T. The stem of the

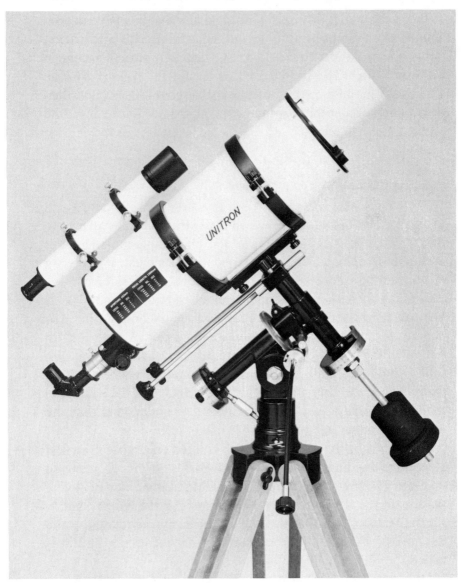

The setting circles can be clearly seen on this German-type equatorial mounting. This telescope is a 4-inch refractor of unusual design. It is an instrument with a 1,500-mm focal length in a tube much shorter than a refractor of conventional design. *(Courtesy Unitron Instruments Inc.)*

T is the polar axis that points at the North Star. The telescope it-self is attached to one end of the T crossbar. A weighted object is put at the other end of the crossbar of the T to balance the weight of the telescope. The crossbar of the T is called the *decli-nation axis* which is essentially up and down. Where the stem of the T meets the crossbar, the mounting swivels around on its polar axis.

The first thing you do with a telescope on an equatorial mount-ing is to adjust the tilt so that it corresponds to the latitude of your location. You only have to do this once, unless you move to another latitude. The easiest way to do this is to call some agency, such as the weather bureau, and ask about your exact latitude. That way is also more accurate than sighting on the North Star. The North Star is about one degree off from true north and it is often difficult to find, especially in cities where there are street lights and air pollution. The next thing to do is to move the telescope along the declination axis (up and down), until it is pointing at the star or planet you want to look at, and lock it there. Now, all you have to do to keep the object in view is to move the instrument along the polar axis.

Setting circles are attached to both the polar and declination axes. These setting circles are marked off in degrees. The mark-ings on the polar-axis setting circle are generally referred to as *hours,* divided into minutes and seconds. The setting circle on the polar axis is generally called the *hour circle.* While the mounting is not a clock, the movement of the polar axis does correspond to the spin of the Earth on its axis, and that follows a general east-west direction. It is the spin of the Earth on its axis that determines what time it is. As the Earth spins, the time changes. The polar axis of the equatorial mounting turns in a di-rection essentially opposite to the direction of the spin of the Earth. In so doing, it keeps the telescope pointed to what you are looking at. You could compare it to looking at an object from a moving train or plane. Suppose, as the train starts out, you are looking out of the side window at an interesting building directly in front of you. Say that the train starts up and moves east. In order to keep your eyes on the building as the train moves east, you have to move your head in a westerly direction.

The movement of the polar axis corresponds to the lines of *longitude.* Another term you will come across in talking about the settings of the polar axis is *right ascension.* The right ascension (hour) settings on the polar axis correspond to the Earth's longitude.

So, all you need to do to keep the star or planet in view with an equatorial mounting is to move the telescope along the polar axis with a slow-motion control. Most good telescopes are equipped with a knob attached to flexible cables for controlling the movement of the telescope along both the polar and declination axes. For more money, you can equip the telescope with a *clock drive.* The clock drive is a motor that moves the telescope on its polar axis at the right speed to keep the star or planet in view. You don't have to turn any knobs, so you can concentrate completely on viewing. Some run on electric motors while others are run by weights, an arrangement that makes them similar to old-fashioned clocks. Many telescope users say that the weight-driven (actually, gravity-driven) clock drives are better than electric clock drives. Electrical current can vary, changing the speed of the drive – not by much, but by enough to bother particular amateur astronomers. Gravity does not vary (maybe it will vary over billions of years, but certainly not in the few hours you use your telescope). A clock drive is most useful for astrophotography.

Supports

The stand on which the telescope and mounting rest is also an important matter. Mounting and stand together provide the support for the telescope. Telescopes are usually sold with a three-legged stand, or *tripod,* made of wood or metal. Tripods can be adequate but a permanent, heavy pier, or base, is better still. For most of us, however, that is not convenient. A permanently mounted telescope has to be protected. It can't be left out in the open all the time. Many amateur astronomers do build or buy "houses" for their telescopes. These range from very expensive domed observatories, with electrically controlled domes that slide open and swing around on tracks, to simple shacks put together from scrap lumber.

However, if you live in a place such as a city or a heavily wooded area, you will have to move the telescope to a place where the viewing is good, where there are no buildings or trees to obstruct your view. The sturdiness of the tripod, then, becomes a very important matter to you. You want to be able to move the telescope, mounting, and tripod conveniently. Unfortunately, convenience and sturdiness do not often go together. For example, many tripods have legs that collapse or slide, to shorten for carrying. That is convenient but any joint or moveable part of the tripod leg weakens it. On the other hand, if you can't shorten the tripod legs in some way, you might have to buy a pickup truck just to move your telescope.

Generally, tripods made of good hardwood, such as oak, are more sturdy than those made of metal rods or tubes. Nevertheless, there are some excellent metal-leg tripods. The best way to find out how good the tripod is, is to try it. If at all possible, set up the telescope at a fairly windy time outside the store where you are shopping. Does the wind make the telescope shake and quiver? You may not notice any shake or quiver until you look through the telescope. Adjust the position of the telescope while looking through it. Does adjusting the telescope position make the image shake and bounce around? How long does it take for the image to "settle down" after you change the position of the instrument?

Some of the smaller "folded optics" telescopes can be used without a tripod or other support. Many of these telescopes can be put on a tabletop or on the hood of a car or on just about anything. Equatorial mountings for these telescopes can be compact and easy to use.

Making Your Own Telescope

Making your own telescope can be a rewarding and money-saving activity. Just how much money you can save over the cost of a factory-made telescope is a matter of how much time you want to spend on your telescope-making project.

Thousands of people have made their own telescopes. Almost all homemade telescopes are reflectors. While it is not impossible to make your own refractor, it would be a far more difficult task than making a reflector. There are two basic ways to make your telescope: (1) start from "scratch" or (2) assemble from ready-made parts or components.

"Scratch" is an appropriate word to use in connection with making a mirror for a reflector. Making a reflector from scratch involves grinding the surface of a glass disk until it has the right degree of curve to collect light. What you want to avoid is scratching the surface.

Grinding a mirror is not particularly difficult but it is tedious and it requires enormous concentration and patience. You start off with two disks of glass. One will be the mirror and the other is the grinding tool. Experienced mirror grinders say that one of the best working "benches" is a cylindrical drum—the kind used to store oil or chemicals. The glass disk that is to be the mirror is securely fixed to the top of the drum with an adhesive. This arrangement allows the worker to walk around the drum, thereby easily getting at all parts of the work. Grinding powders (abrasives) are put on the disk and the glass tool is moved over the disk in a circular pattern to grind the surface. Actually, very little glass has to be removed to get the surface to the right shape but that shape has to be just right, so the work has to be done very carefully and slowly. Don't try too big a mirror for your first attempt. A six-inch mirror is a good size for a first try.

It seems reasonable enough to ask, "How do you know when

the surface is the right shape?" There are a number of simple tests for correct surface shape that can be done without elaborate equipment. These tests are among the more detailed information on telescope making you will find in the many books on the subject.

After the mirror is correctly ground, polished, and silvered, you have the choice of how much of the rest of the telescope you will make yourself and how much you will buy ready-made.

Assembling a telescope from components is also a rewarding activity. The advantage is that you can have a telescope ready to use much more quickly than you could by grinding your own mirror. Mirrors, tubes, mirror holders, eyepieces, focusing mechanisms, mountings, tripods, and more, are all available from many suppliers. You could make some of these parts, too, but some are more difficult to make than others. It would be extremely difficult, for example, to make an eyepiece, but making an equatorial mounting is not only possible, it is also a very interesting thing to do. You can also make your own support or tripod.

Most amateurs, who make their own telescopes today, do so by assembling parts. However, you might find that you really like to grind mirrors. If you get good at it, for a few hundred dollars you could make a telescope that would cost $5,000 or more if bought completely assembled.

If you are thinking about making a refractor, forget about grinding your own lenses. The equipment needed for grinding the lenses would probably cost more than a ready-made telescope. You can buy object lenses, tubes, and so on. However, unless you have a collection of tools and equipment that amounts to a small machine shop, you might have a difficult time assembling a refractor.

Buying a Microscope

Finding a place to buy a microscope can be as much a problem as finding a place to buy a telescope. For the same reasons as mentioned for telescopes, there is not likely to be a large selection of microscopes in department and discount stores. Some hobby and camera stores may carry some microscopes but, again, the selection is not likely to be great.

There is no widely available magazine, such as *Sky and Telescope*, in which you will find ads from companies that sell microscopes designed for use by amateurs. Of course, there are magazines for scientists, such as *Science*, but the microscopes advertised there are likely to be very elaborate and expensive. However, you can look through issues of *Science*, then write to the companies that advertise microscopes and ask them for a catalogue. Tell them you are just starting out and are interested in microscopes for beginners. Magazines for science teachers, such as *The Science Teacher*, will also have ads for microscopes, and many of those advertised in the magazine might be the right kind for you.

If you live in or around a fairly large city, chances are you will find a "Microscopes" listing in the Yellow Pages of the telephone book. You would have to live in a much bigger city to find a "Telescopes" listing in the Yellow Pages. The reason is that many businesses and industries use microscopes, while few have much use for telescopes. Calling one of those places listed under microscopes in the Yellow Pages just could get you some help in finding a microscope suitable for you. So, as is the case with telescopes, if you live in a small town, chances are that you will have to buy your microscope by mail order.

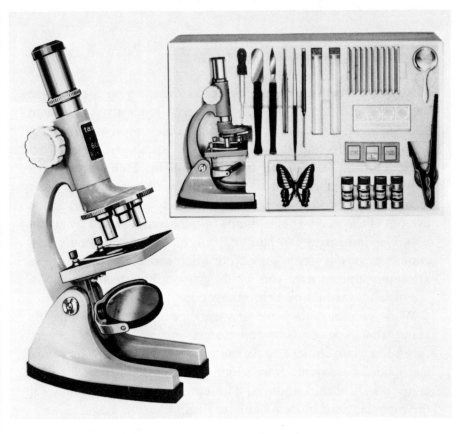

This microscope is supplied in a kit with slides and dissecting instruments. *(Courtesy Tasco Sales)*

What to Look for in a Microscope

Buying a microscope can be easier than buying a telescope because there are not as many different kinds from which to choose. While there are actually many different kinds of microscopes, the only kind that will be of much use to you is a light microscope that works with transmitted light. Unless you have more money than you know what to do with, you are not likely to buy an electron microscope. Also, you would not get much use out of the many special kinds of microscopes used by scientists and industries for hundreds of special tasks. You might choose to buy a stereo-dissecting microscope, but while these are interesting to use, you would get much more use out of a "regular" transmission light microscope.

While you may not have to spend too much time pondering about what type of microscope to get, you will have to be very careful in your choice. As is the case with anything, there are many fine instruments from which to choose, but there are also many poorly made products. The latter might make money for the manufacturer but are likely to disappoint the buyer.

The two main things to look for are optical quality and mechanical quality. The best way to judge both optical and mechanical quality is to use the microscope. There are things about the way the microscope is made that can tell you something about the optical quality even before you look through it. A "full size" microscope with "full size" objectives is likely to give better results than are most of the smaller microscopes offered to hobbyists. "Full size" means a microscope that is at least twelve inches high and has objectives around a half inch in diameter. Remember that this statement is a generality. You can find a full-sized piece of junk too; on the other hand, there are many well-made smaller microscopes.

Looking through the microscope can tell you a few things

about both the optical and mechanical quality. Look through the microscope, making sure there is enough light going into the instrument, either from a built-in light source or from an outside light source and a mirror. If the microscope has more than one objective, try one of the middle powers first. Bring the microscope into focus. The focusing mechanism is usually controlled by a knob. When you move the knob, the tube of the microscope should move smoothly but firmly (some microscopes are focused by moving the stage rather than the microscope tube). The best focusing arrangement is rack and pinion. Adjust the focus until you get the sharpest image. Now, let go of the knob and keep looking into the microscope. Does the image stay in, or drift out of, focus? Drifting out of focus is an indication of poor construction, that is, poor mechanical quality.

Better microscopes have at least two adjusting knobs, a larger one for coarse adjustment and a smaller one for fine adjustment. The coarse adjustment is for getting the image approximately into focus and the fine adjustment is for more precise focusing. If the microscope you are thinking of buying has a fine adjustment, be sure to also check the fine adjustment for drift.

Now, with the microscope at the sharpest possible focus you can get for the middle-power range, switch to a higher power. If the microscope has more than one objective, it will most probably have a revolving turret on which the objectives are mounted. Swing it around to the next highest power. Make sure it is completely in place.

Look into the microscope. Is the image in or out of focus? Better microscopes are *parfocal*. That is, if it is in focus for one power, it will be in focus (except for very fine adjustment) for any other power (some may not be parfocal for all the objectives).

How clear can you get the high-power image? Does it stay fuzzy no matter how hard you try to get it to focus? If that is the case, the lenses are probably of poor quality. What about light? Is the image dull and on the dark side? Try increasing the light.

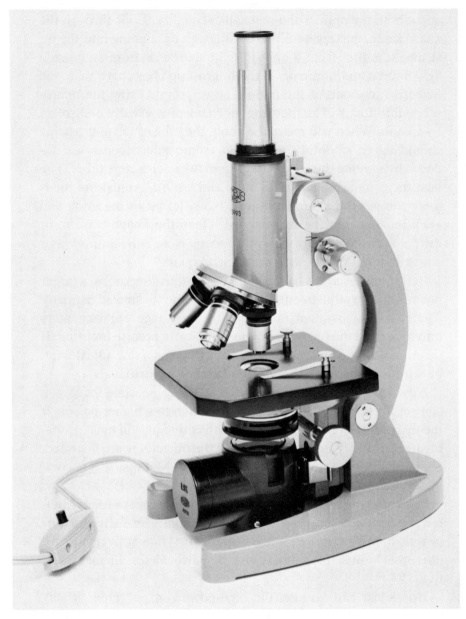

This student microscope has a condenser and iris diaphragm. *(Courtesy Olympus Corporation of America)*

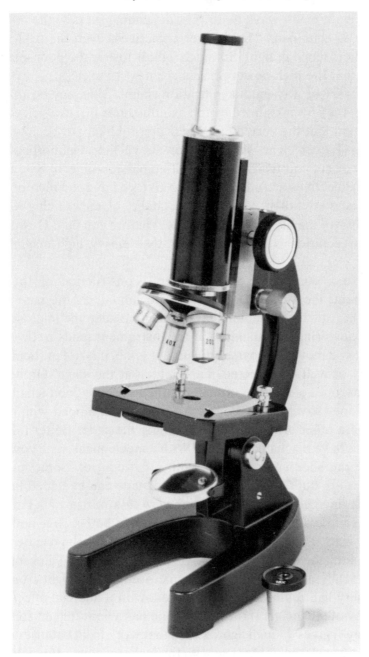

This is a relatively low-cost instrument that has a fine adjustment and a disk diaphragm. *(Courtesy Edmund Scientific Company)*

(There are many ways to do this, depending on how the microscope is equipped.) High-power objectives, even the best, rob the microscope of light. So much light is lost in the poor-quality ones that the high-power images are next to useless.

Be wary of way-out magnification claims. You may be able to obtain the power claimed by the manufacturer in a low-priced instrument, but the very high powers are not likely to be good for much. To get clear, sharp images above the neighborhood of 800× or so, you really need an oil-immersion objective. Undersized objectives are not as likely to give you as good high-power images as are full-sized objectives, quality of lenses being equal. Always try the highest-claimed power before you buy. However, good resolution is more important than empty high magnifications.

Take a good look at the general construction of the instrument. Pick it up. Does it feel substantial? Is the base (the part that sits on the table) heavy enough to keep the microscope from quivering and shaking? If the instrument tends to tip over when you move the coarse adjustment knob, it is not particularly heavy or well constructed. Take a look at the stage. On better microscopes it is made of metal, although some good small microscopes have plastic stages. It should be equipped with clips or some other arrangement for holding the slide. Better microscopes have mechanical stages. With a mechanical stage you can move the slide smoothly and with great control. Some microscopes are built so that a mechanical stage can be added later.

The microscope may be equipped with a mirror or a built-in light source. One side of the mirror should be *concave* and the other side *plane* (straight). The mirror types can be used either with sunlight or with a lamp. It is best to use a light source specifically made for use with a microscope. The light from an ordinary light bulb has too much yellow in it and can affect the quality of the image. If the microscope has a built-in light source, be sure it gives enough light. Types that work from batteries may not give enough light for use with the higher powers. If you buy a

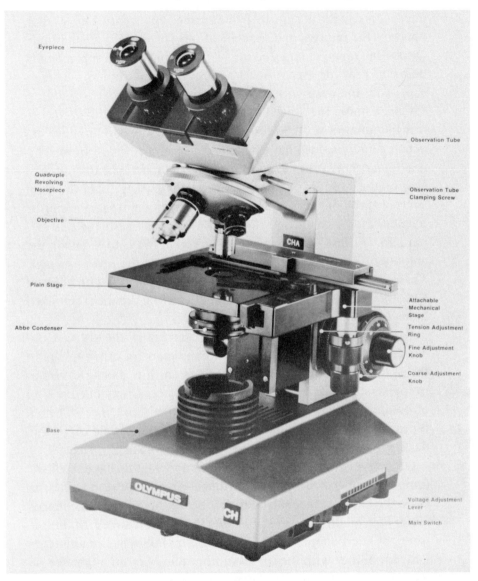

This research-quality microscope has a mechanical stage. *(Courtesy Olympus Corporation of America)*

microscope with a built-in light source, buy spare bulbs when you buy the microscope. Specifications for these built-in illuminators can change, and you might be unable to find replacement bulbs a year or two after you buy the instrument. This is especially the case with imported microscopes.

Check under the stage to see what there is, if anything, to control the amount of light entering the microscope. The more expensive microscopes have what is called an *iris diaphragm*. This is a device similar to the aperture control on better cameras. The size of the hole through which the light passes from the light source, through the specimen, and into the microscope can be opened widely or closed down to a pinpoint with the iris diaphragm. A less expensive but effective way to control the amount of light going through the specimen is the *revolving disk*. This is a circular piece of material (metal or plastic) with holes of various sizes in it. The disk is rotated to bring the different-sized holes into position.

Better microscopes have a condenser under the stage. Condensers concentrate the light and can do many other things to the light, depending upon the user's need. For example, bacteriologists, those scientists who study bacteria, may need a kind of condenser that produces an effect called *dark field*. Certain types of bacteria show up best if the surrounding field of view is dark. Other types of condensers produce *phase contrast*.

Objectives on better-quality microscopes should have the N.A. (numerical aperture) written on them. Remember, the lower the N.A. the better (especially at higher powers), provided the lenses are of high quality and the objective is assembled well. Manufacturers of microscopes intended for use by hobbyists or amateurs may not bother with the NA. Another number you might see on the objective is the *working distance* given in millimeters. This is the distance between the tip of the objective and the slide, when the image is in focus. The higher the power, the·less the working distance.

Better-quality microscopes are equipped with automatic stops

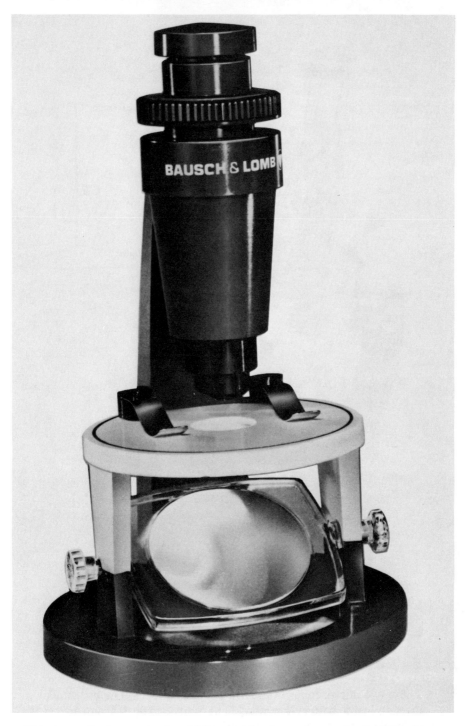

This type of microscope is widely used in elementary schools. Easy to use, it is a first microscope for many hobbyists. *(Courtesy Bausch and Lomb)*

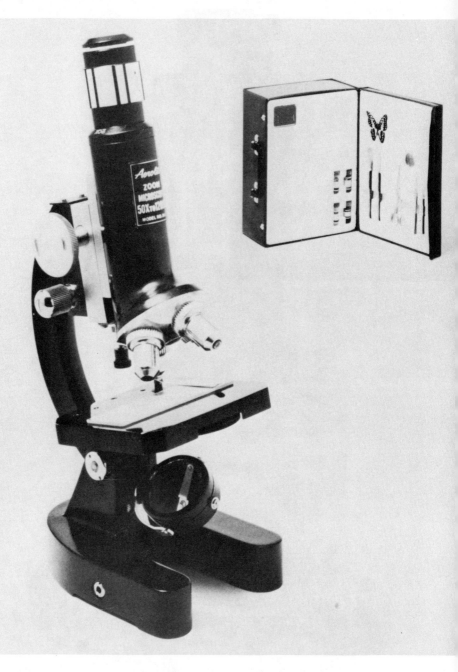

These two microscopes both have zoom eyepieces. The instrument on the left has a battery-operated light source. The instrument on the right, designed for use in schools, has a single objective. *(Courtesy Swift Instruments, Boston, Massachusetts)*

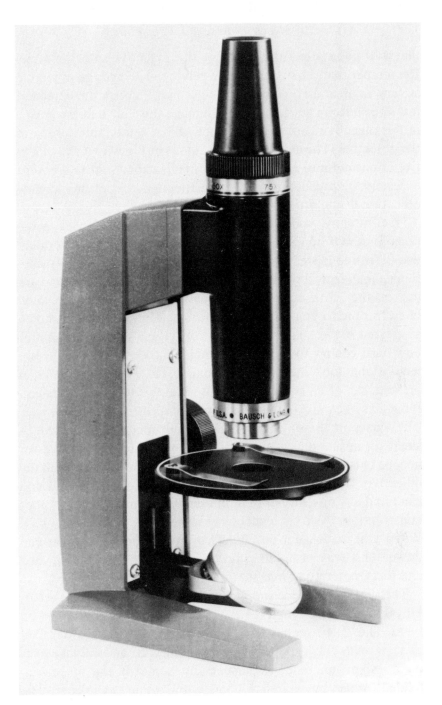

(*Courtesy Bausch and Lomb*)

that will keep you from jamming the objective into the slide. Remember that the distance between the slide and the objective is very small at high powers. It is not hard to push the objective into the slide, an action that can damage the slide and the lenses in the objective. Some microscopes have retractable lenses in the objective. These will move back out of the way if the objective is pushed into a slide. As you might expect, these are very expensive and you can do without the high cost of this kind of objective if you are careful.

Occasionally, you might find that there are bad lenses in the objectives. Of course, the manufacturer does not deliberately use defective lenses but they can get by inspectors, and sometimes the defects develop after the objective and microscope are put together. Pits, cracks, and air bubbles in the lenses are some of the problems you might come across. These problems can be suspected if the image is cloudy, fuzzy, and uneven no matter how hard you try to bring it into focus. You can remove the objective and look into the open end of it. Pits and cracks, if present, can often be seen with this kind of inspection. A magnifying glass helps. Another problem is improperly placed lenses. The lenses in the objective must be put together just right. A slight tilt in just one of the lenses is enough to result in a poor image. This kind of defect is not too easy to find by looking at the objective. If the performance of the objective is poor and you can't find any pits, air bubbles, or cracks, you might suspect poor construction. Ask to inspect the objectives before you buy. When you do inspect an objective, hold it with the open end down. This way of holding the objective helps to prevent dust and dirt from getting into it.

The type of eyepiece supplied with most microscopes is a 10× Huygenian. Some eyepieces have the letters "WF" stamped on them. The "WF" means wide field; that is, you get a wider field of view with this type of eyepiece than with an ordinary eyepiece. Some microscopes, especially some of the makes intended for use by amateurs, come with "zoom" eyepieces. The

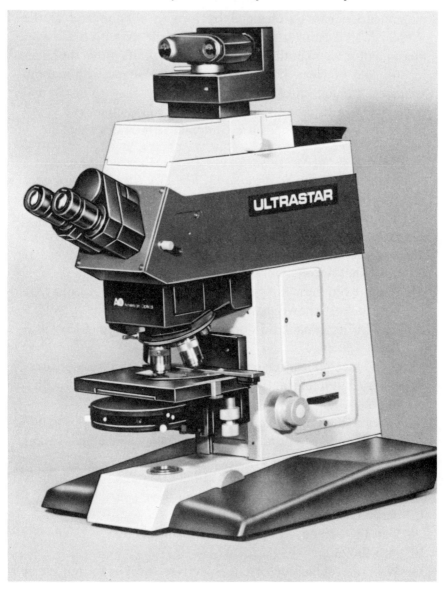

A well-equipped research-quality microscope. *(Courtesy American Optical Corporation)*

magnification can be changed by turning a knob around the eyepiece. You can get some interesting effects with these eye-pieces, but remember that the higher the magnification, the smaller the field of view. If you do buy a microscope with a zoom eyepiece, treat it carefully. They are fairly easy to break and once they are broken, repairing them is very expensive. Very few research microscopes are equipped with zoom eyepieces.

Questions to Ask the Salesperson When You Buy a Microscope:
1. Are the lenses in the objectives and eyepiece achromatic and coated?
2. Are the lenses made of glass?
3. Are the working distances stamped on the objectives? If not, what are the working distances?
4. Are the Numerical Apertures stamped on the objectives? If not, do you know what they are?
5. Can I bring it back if I don't like it? How long can I try it to see if I like it?
6. Can a mechanical stage be added later? (Not absolutely necessary, but important if you intend to do serious work with a microscope.)
7. Does it have a condenser? Is the condenser achromatic? Can a condenser be added later? Are they available if I want to add one later?
8. (For microscopes with built-in light sources.) How long is the bulb expected to last? Do you have spare bulbs that I can buy right now if I buy the microscope?
9. Can the objectives be removed for inspection?
10. Are the objectives parfocal?
11. Will you replace defective objectives, eyepieces, lenses, et cetera?
12. Is there an automatic stop to prevent jamming an objective into the slide?

Using Your Telescope

Although when you get your new telescope the first thing you will want to do is take it outside and use it, don't do anything until you read the instruction book that comes with the instrument. Usually some assembly is necessary and some adjustments will always have to be made before your telescope is ready to be used.

You might be thinking that you will use your telescope only at night. While it is true that most of the beautiful things there are to be looked at in the heavens can be seen only at night, there is much daytime use for your telescope. It can be used to look at things in this world, too. For example, you can see faraway animals, mountain peaks, and many other interesting things as you have never seen them before. Of course, the image you get with an astronomical telescope will be upside down, but many telescopes come with an *erecting prism.* The erecting prism turns the image right side up. It also robs you of light, but that doesn't matter too much when you are using the telescope for making general observations. The Sun lights up things effectively enough. Remember, though, that an astronomical telescope is designed for looking at sky objects. It has some limitations for general use, such as a narrow field of view compared to telescopes designed for just looking around.

While you can put your telescope to daytime use, there is, however, one daytime object that requires a special caution and that is the Sun. **Do not look directly at the sun with a telescope, binoculars, or any optical instrument not specifically equipped for solar observation.** If you have ever used a magnifying glass to start a fire, you know what can happen. A telescope gathers and concentrates light. The light from the Sun so gathered and concentrated could burn the retina of your eye in less than a second. All of these warnings do not mean that you cannot use your telescope to observe the Sun. You can, but you must do so in the safe, approved way.

Many people using a telescope for the first time are disappointed because they don't always get clear, crisp, bright images every time. Being disappointed the first few times you use a telescope is like being disappointed because you can't play a violin concerto the first time you pick up a violin. You have to learn how to play the violin and, similarly, you have to learn how to use a telescope. You will be happy to know that learning how to use a telescope is not a fraction as difficult as learning how to play the violin. You don't need to take lessons to use a telescope, but pointers and advice from an experienced telescope user are always welcome. There are many beautiful things to see in the heavens and the more you use your telescope, the more you will learn and the more you will see.

Difficulties in seeing are not necessarily the fault of the telescope. The atmosphere provides most of the problems. As pointed out before, the atmosphere is constantly moving about and changing. Some layers of atmosphere are hot and others are cold. These temperature differences set up seething, churning air currents. The light from the star or planet you are looking at has to pass through all that before it gets to your telescope and your eye. Additional problems can come from pollution, heat, and light in cities. Seeing tends to get worse closer to the horizon, and better, higher up from the horizon.

Some nights are better for observation than others. For example, you know that a cloudy night with or without rain is just no good for using an astronomical telescope. You certainly can't see anything, and the rain will do your telescope no good. Not all clear nights are good observation nights, either. Generally, cold, clear nights are better than warm or hot nights. Cold air tends to be quieter than heated air. Of course you don't want to go out when it's ten or twenty degrees below zero. Such cold temperatures could harm both you and your telescope. However, many of the best viewing nights do occur when the temperature is below freezing, so dress accordingly. Experienced telescope users soon learn how to handle eyepieces and focusing knobs with gloved or mittened hands. Wear a hat and earmuffs, too, and protect your feet with wool socks and shoes or boots designed for cold-weather use. Nothing will drive you indoors faster than cold, aching feet.

Some warm nights might surprise you. Conditions usually get better later at night. In the early evening hours, the ground starts to give up some of the heat that accumulated during the day. The radiation of heat from the ground sets up air currents at just about the level of the telescope. However, as the temperature of the air and ground begin to even out, these air currents slow down. So be patient on those summer evenings. For example, early in the evening Jupiter might look like a yellow pea floating in a big caldron of steaming chicken soup, but a few hours later it could be clear, crisp, and beautiful to behold. On warm nights set up your telescope on grass rather than pavement if you can. Pavement gives up heat more rapidly than grass, so the air around grass is likely to be quieter than the air over concrete or asphalt. With experience you will soon learn which nights are worth staying up for, and, like a fisherman who finds the best fishing spots, you will find the best viewing spots.

You can use your telescope for direct viewing or taking pictures. Generally, the lenses of the telescope rather than those of the camera are used. Most telescope manufacturers sell cameras specifically designed for use with their telescopes. However, with the use of adapter rings and tubes, almost any good camera can be attached to a telescope. Most better camera stores sell this kind of equipment. Astrophotography can be a rewarding activity, but you must have patience. A lot of experimenting is needed to determine the best exposure times, apertures, film types, and so on. So be prepared to go through quite a bit of film before you get satisfactory results.

The Moon

The Moon will probably be the first thing you will look at with your telescope. And, indeed, it should be. You are not likely to be disappointed. The Moon is easy to find in the night sky (and sometimes in the daytime sky). It is a rewarding object to look at with the smallest telescope or even a pair of binoculars. On poor viewing nights, when practically nothing else is worth looking at, the Moon will almost always come through.

Contrary to what you might think, telescope users, including professional astronomers, never get tired of looking at the Moon. You are not likely to discover anything about it that is not already known and, except for the footprints and assorted hardware left there and the rocks removed by astronauts, the surface has not changed for millions of years. However, your view of the Moon is always changing. As the position of the Earth and Moon changes in relation to the Sun, the light from the Sun strikes the Moon at different angles, and the angle at which you view the Moon changes. The changing patterns of light and shadow can give you a new view every night. You will see things in that crater or on that mountaintop you didn't see the night before.

The full Moon is not the best observation time. For one thing, the light from a full Moon is so bright that it can actually hurt your eyes to look at it through a telescope. Some of the best observations are made by concentrating on the terminator—the line between light and darkness on the Moon. The glare is not severe at the terminator, and the shadows often help to bring out features that are lost in the bright light of a full Moon.

Following are some suggestions on how to use the terminator to get the most out of your observations. The features discussed here are only a few of the many interesting things there are to see on the Moon. The distances and heights given are approximations. Most of the features can be seen with a three-inch refractor or a six-inch reflector. Some can be seen with smaller telescopes or binoculars. As is the case with all observations made with your telescope, it is usually best to start with a low power to get as wide a field of view as possible for scanning. When you find something that interests you, you can try higher powers to study the feature in detail.

The Crescent Moon. Don't think there is nothing to see when the moon is new—that is, just a crescent. There is much to see. The best time to start your "tour" is about three days after the new Moon. The Sea of Crises (Mare Crisium) shows up beautifully at this time. This is one of the smaller "seas" and is usually not noticed when the Moon is full. Of course, the "seas" are not really seas. There is no water on the Moon. To early observers, these relatively flat areas looked like oceans. The names of the seas reflect the imagination of the early observers; other features are named after famous people, such as astronomers.

Surrounded by some impressive mountains, the Sea of Crises is definitely worth looking at. Some interesting craters and other features are visible on the crescent Moon. Among these are the 160-kilometer (100 mile)-wide crater, Petavius. Larger "craters," such as Furnerius, are also called *walled plains*. These are flat areas surrounded by formations that sort of wall them in. Some of these walls rise to spectacular heights, and some observers say that looking at them actually makes them dizzy. Some of the larger walled plains are sometimes called seas. The walls of Furnerius are 3,350 meters (11,000 feet) high. To the north (remember, your image is upside down; north is "down") are two more walled plains. Parts of the wall of one of these walled plains, Cleomedes, are 4,876 meters (16,000 feet) high. Cleomedes lies just to the north of the Sea of Crises, and it has an interesting mountain in its center. Farther north is Endymion, a walled plain with a dark floor that seems to change in color as the Moon "expands."

Five to Six Days. As the Moon continues to *lunate* (that is, expand), the Sea of Fertility comes into view. There are a number of small craters in the sea, including the "twin" craters Messier and Pickering. They lie close together in the approximate center of the sea. A whitish double streak sticks out more or less in an easterly direction from Pickering. For years, one of the ongoing arguments among astronomers was "Which of the twins, if any, is the bigger one?" Messier is the larger, but many amateurs see Pickering as larger. This effect is one type of the many optical illusions caused by shadows.

To the east of the Sea of Fertility is a string, or chain, of three craters — Theophilus, Cyrillus, and Catharina. The walls of Theophilus are 5,140 meters (18,000 feet) high. The sea that is seen at this time is the Sea of Tranquillity. This sea is the site of the July 20, 1969, landing of Apollo 11, the first manned mission to the moon. However, you will not be able to see the lunar lander or the footprints made by the first people to walk on the moon.

Seven Days: The First Quarter or Half-Moon. Many amateur astronomers will tell you that half-Moon is the absolutely best time to look at the Moon through a telescope. Many say they get the feeling that they are right there on that silent, silvery world. Hundreds of craters are visible, and the observer is tempted to linger on one of them, studying the details of the walls and the floor. A three-inch refractor or six-inch reflector should enable you to see the Hyginus cleft, a one-mile-wide, 240-kilometer (150 mile)-long strip that appears to be a fault or crack in the surface. It is actually a string of tiny craterlets. A larger crater, the 6.15-kilometer (four mile)-wide Hyginus, is found in the approximate midway point of the apparent cleft.

The Sea of Serenity (Mare Serenitatis) is one of the larger

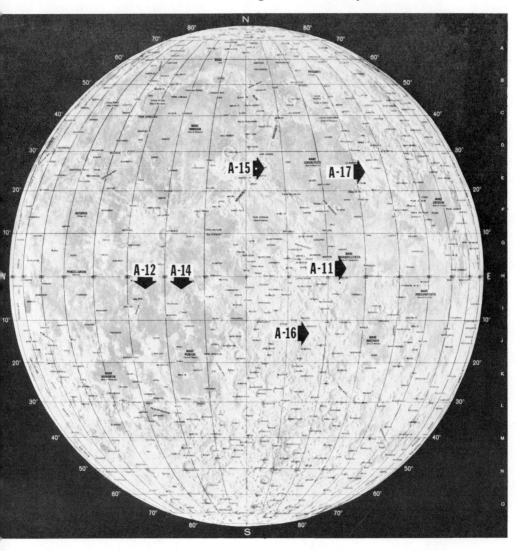

A photographic moon map showing the Apollo landing sites. Use this
map to follow the day-by-day moon observations. *(NASA)*

seas. At the southern and eastern edges are some spectacular mountain ranges — the Haemus, Caucasus, and (the most magnificent of all) the Apennine Range which continues into the dark half of the Moon. The floor of the Sea of Serenity appears to be very smooth, but careful observation will reveal a few ridges. Two large craters, Aristotle and Eudoxus, are at the northern edge of the Mare.

Nine to Ten Days. Some of the more spectacular walled plains are now visible. These are called Ptolemaeus, Alphonsus, and Arzachel. In 1958, a Russian astronomer, Nikolai Kozyrev, using a fifty-inch reflector, reported seeing a reddish glow and a puff of gas coming out of a mountain in Alphonsus. This observation suggested that a volcanic eruption had taken place. However, other observers had reported seeing glows and flashes there before. But the "volcanic eruption" may be another example of an optical illusion caused by the play of light across the different shades of color on the floor of the plain. Nevertheless, many astronomers believe it was, indeed, a volcanic eruption. You might want to pay special attention to this area. Keep in mind that any eruption you might see with a small telescope would have to be enormous.

The large crater Tycho, 86.9 kilometers (54 miles) across, is in view now. There are some impressive mountains inside the crater, and the crater has an extensive system of rays that radiate out from it for considerable distances. To the south of Tycho is the magnificent Clavius, 230 kilometers (145 miles) across. There are more craters arranged in a rather neat row on its floor. The Sea of Clouds (Mare Nubium) is north of Clavius. Near the Sea of Clouds is a 96-kilometer (60 mile)-long ridge called the Straight Wall. The Straight Wall is bordered on the south by a branching pattern of mountains called the Stag's Horn Mountains.

Many moon watchers regard the crater Copernicus to be the most spectacular feature on the lunar surface. The approximate

At half-moon is considered to be the best time to observe the moon.
(*Courtesy Meade Instruments Corporation Inc.*)

half-Moon brings out the best in this large, 90-kilometer (56 mile)-wide crater. When the terminator is right on Copernicus, it fills with shadow and, according to many observers, it seems as though you could reach out and grab it. The walls of Copernicus are 5,180 meters (17,000 feet) high. The inner surface of the walls are terraced. Three separate mountain peaks are located inside the crater.

To the south is the Fra Mauro crater near the landing site of Apollo 14. A little to the west are the Apennine Mountains which include a 6,085-meter (20,000 feet) peak, Mount Huygens. The Alps, which are to the north of the Apennines, are made interesting by a feature that looks like a giant knife cut slashing a straight line through the hills.

The Sea of Rains (Mare Imbrium) is bordered on the west by the Apennines. Plato, a dark-floored walled plain, is on the northern rim of the Sea of Rains. It is 96 kilometers (60 miles) wide and has many craterlets scattered about on its floor. They are not easy to see, and picking them out is a challenge to the owners of small (three-inch refractor, six-inch reflector, and slightly larger) instruments. The mountain peak to the south of Plato is Pico. The Bay of Rainbows (Sinus Iridum) to the east of Plato is particularly beautiful when the terminator passes through it. If you look at just the right time, you will see a crescent-shaped, shining mountain range.

Eleven to Twelve Days. The bright carter Kepler is visible at this time. It has an interesting "burstlike" ray system. To the north, Aristarchus, the brightest crater on the Moon, is the feature to look for at this time. Early astronomers were convinced that huge volcanic eruptions were taking place there, but the "eruptions" are tricks played on the eye by the brightness of this crater. Aristarchus is 46 kilometers (29 miles) wide. The brightness comes from a deposit of whitish material that is highly reflective, almost like a mirror. A small, but bright, ray system is in the center. The mountain peak in the center is so bright that filters are needed on large telescopes to cut down the glare. Over the years, observers have reported violet and orange glows in the crater.

Aristarchus is an example of a *banded crater*. After the sun rises over the crater, two or three bands can be seen running from the central mountain toward the eastern wall. These bands appear to get longer and darker through the lunar day (27.3 Earth days). It is not known whether these changes in the bands are real or an optical illusion. Studying these bands is one example of a long-range Moon-observation project.

Schroter's Valley lies to the north of Aristarchus. It is a U-shaped valley that runs in a northerly direction for about thirty miles and then switches back in a southeasterly direction. This valley is a real fault and not a chain of craters. The crater Gassendi, 88 kilometers (55 miles) across, is seen at this time. It is at the northern edge of the Sea of Moisture (Mare Humorum). The floor has an interesting pattern of clefts. This crater is another area that has been watched for signs of volcanic activity.

Thirteen Days to Full. Some very large craters are the major attractions at this time. Grimaldi is 192 kilometers (120 miles) across and has a low mountain range inside the walls. A companion crater, Riccioli, is only slightly smaller. To the south are the Rook Mountains. Some 6,095-meter (20,000 feet) peaks are in this mountain range. Farther south is Schickard, a huge walled plain, only a little smaller than Clavius. After fourteen days, the Moon begins to wane and you can repeat your tour in the other direction.

The Other Side of the Moon. You probably know that only one "side" of the Moon is visible to an observer on Earth. The reason for this frustrating state of affairs is found in the way the Moon revolves around the Earth and the way the Moon spins on its axis.

The Moon revolves around the Earth in a counterclockwise

direction. You also probably know that the month is based on the time it takes for the Moon to complete one revolution. There are two kinds of Moon months—the *synodic* and the *sidereal*. The synodic month is 29.53 days. It is the average period of time between one alignment of the Earth, Moon, and Sun and the next alignment. The sidereal month is based on the period between the time the Earth and Moon are in line, with a star used as a reference point, and the next time the Earth and Moon are so aligned. The reason the synodic month is longer is that while the Moon revolves around the Earth, it is also moving around the Sun. The Moon has to move a little more to catch up before the Earth, Moon, and Sun are in line again.

While the Moon is going around the Earth, it is also spinning on its axis in a counterclockwise direction. The Moon makes a complete rotation on its axis in 27.32 days. That period of time, therefore, is "one day" on the Moon. Note that the rotation period is approximately the same as the time it takes the Moon to go around the Earth. This combination of movement means that the same side of the Moon is always facing the Earth.

However, the division between the part you can see from Earth and the part you can't see is not an even fifty-fifty. Effects called *librations* make it possible for you to see more than half the Moon's surface, but not all at the same time. Librations are apparent "nodding," or up-and-down and side-to-side, motions of the side of the Moon facing the Earth. The Moon isn't really nodding. As the Moon and Earth spin and rotate, the angles at which we view the Moon change, causing the librations. The librations are side to side (east to west) and up and down (north to south). The result is that 41 percent of the Moon is always visible, 41 percent is never visible, and 18 percent is sometimes visible and sometimes not, depending on the librations. Also, two observers at widely separated points would have slightly different views of the Moon. After several weeks of experience in observing, you should be able to notice the difference in how much of the Moon is showing at any given time.

An *eclipse* of the Moon occurs when the Earth passes between the Sun and Moon, and the Earth's shadow falls on the Moon. Eclipses of the Moon can be very interesting to observe with your telescope. Use a low power so you can get as much into your field of view as possible. Studying the Moon's features as the Earth's shadow moves across the surface can be fascinating. Temperatures on the lunar surface drop sharply as the shadow moves across. Sudden drops in temperature from the boiling point of water down to less than $-75°C$ ($-100°$ F) can produce some interesting effects.

Occultations are also interesting to observe. An occultation occurs when the Moon passes "in front" of a star or planet and blocks your view of it. The star or planet seems to go out like a turned-off electric light as the Moon crosses it. Many observers think that occultations of planets are more spectacular than occultations of stars.

The Sun

As far as the inhabitants of this world are concerned, the Sun is the most important star in the universe. As stars go, it is rather puny and second-rate, but it is the ultimate source of life and energy on this planet. Events on the Sun can affect our weather, food supply, and much more. Small wonder that the Sun is the most studied of all the bodies in space.

You can study the Sun, too, but remember that the equipment you have is limited. You must be very careful. **Looking directly at the Sun through an improperly equipped telescope can permanently damage your eyes, possibly causing complete blindness.** The safest way to observe the Sun is to use your telescope to project an image with it. Most refractors come equipped with a Sun projection screen. If your telescope does not have one, you can order or make one yourself. This screen is generally a flat, white piece of metal or some other material. It is attached to a rod which is clamped to the telescope tube forward of the eyepiece. To use the screen, the telescope is directed at the Sun. **Do not look through the telescope while you are trying to get it pointed at the Sun.** Look at the projection on the screen. Bring the image into sharpest focus by moving the focusing mechanism and the screen back and forth. You will have to experiment to find the right distance for the best combination of size and sharpness of image. With a three-inch refractor and an 18-mm eyepiece you should be able to get a Sun image about six inches across. The projected image is not as sharp and detailed as the image you would get looking at the Sun directly, but it is safer and more comfortable than direct observation. Projection is a particularly good way to study sunspots and solar eclipses.

Direct observation is possible with the right equipment. However, it is a good idea to get as much advice as you can from experienced observers before trying it yourself. Solar diagonals, also called solar wedges or Herschel wedges, are used for direct solar observation. A solar wedge, placed in the light path of the telescope, allows only a fraction of the Sun's heat and light to pass through to your eye. It is best to use a solar wedge in conjunction with a solar filter that is placed over the object glass. However, using a solar filter alone for solar observations is not recommended.

Sunspots and other features of the solar surface can be seen with direct observation. Direct viewing with a wedge and filter will reveal the granular nature of the solar surface. The granular part of the Sun you see with your telescope is the *photosphere.* It is a layer of gases about two hundred miles thick.

Sunspots are interesting to look at, and they can be the basis of a long-range viewing and research project. Sunspots are dark areas on the surface of the sun. They have a darker central part called the *umbra* and a lighter outer area called the *penumbra.* They are much cooler than the rest of the Sun, but don't let the word "cool" give you the wrong idea. Although the coolest part of a sunspot is about 1,600° F cooler than the rest of the solar

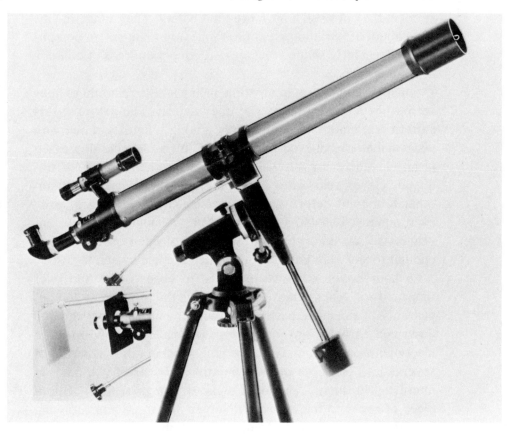

The inset in this picture of a 2.4-inch refractor shows a sun-projection screen set up for use. *(Courtesy Swift Instruments)*

surface, they are still a bit more than balmy. They range in size from about 1,500 kilometers (900 miles) in diameter to complicated, irregularly shaped masses that cover hundreds of millions of square miles.

Sunspots can appear at any time in any number, but there does seem to be a pattern in the way they appear. The nature of this pattern is a matter of controversy among scientists. For many years scientists believed that sunspots increased and decreased in an eleven-year cycle. That is, they reached a peak in frequency eleven years after a low point and then decreased to another low point before again increasing. In recent years, however, some scientists have disputed the existence of an eleven-year cycle, claiming that the Sun has not been observed long enough to say with certainty that such a cycle exists.

Of course, you can't be expected to observe the Sun over thousands of years, but you can observe the movement and appearance of sunspots, particularly with the projection technique described earlier. Sunspots, even the smallest, show up quite nicely with projection. Try observing sunspots over a period of several days or weeks or even months and years if you are that interested in them. You could make drawings of them. Clip a piece of paper to the projection screen and trace your drawing over the projected image. Many sunspot observers use a grid to plot the position of the sunspots. That is, a circle, marked off in squares, like graph paper, is clipped to the projection screen. The position of the sunspots is marked on the grid. Over a period of time, the movements and size changes of the spots can be recorded.

The Sun rotates on its axis, but some parts of it rotate at different speeds. The periods of rotation at the equator is about 25 days. At 40° latitude it is 27.5 days; at polar regions the rate of rotation is even slower. The variable rotation speeds and other factors can make plotting sunspots a difficult and challenging activity. Some excellent techniques for plotting sunspots are described in *The Amateur Astronomer's Handbook* by James Muirden.

When sunspots first begin to appear again, after a period in which few spots are seen, the spots occur mostly in the higher latitudes. The regions of activity seem to move toward the equator as the number of sunspots increase.

The *aurora borealis,* or northern lights, are associated with sunspots. The aurorae are caused by radioactive particles from the Sun entering the Earth's atmosphere. These particles cause the atmosphere at high Earth latitudes to light up somewhat like a neon sign. *Flares,* bright flashes of light that occur near sunspots, send off large amounts of this radiation. The Earth is a magnet and attracts these particles. The Earth's magnetic field, however, keeps the particles away from the Earth's equatorial regions. That is why aurorae are best seen at higher latitudes in the Northern Hemisphere and at lower latitudes in the Southern Hemisphere. The Northern Hemisphere aurorae are usually much more spectacular than those in the Southern Hemisphere. If you should observe a sudden increase in the number of sunspots, you can count on an increase in auroral activity about two days later. If you live too far south to see aurorae, you can check with the weather bureau for information on their occurrence.

Solar eclipses. You may be fortunate enough to be at the right time at the right place to view a solar eclipse. There are few sky shows more spectacular than this one. The last total solar eclipse visible in the United States occurred on February 26, 1979. The next to be visible from points within the United States and Canada will not occur until the next century. On February 16, 1980, a total solar eclipse was visible in Central Africa, China, and India; on July 31, 1981, one will be visible in the Soviet Union; and on June 11, 1983, in the southern Indian Ocean and the western Pacific Ocean. However, on July 11, 1991, a total eclipse will be visible in nearby Central America. This eclipse promises to be a particularly good one. The time of total eclipse will be more than six minutes.

A solar eclipse occurs when the Moon passes between the Sun and the Earth in such a way that the shadow of the Moon falls on the Earth. A solar eclipse does not happen every time the Moon passes the Earth and Sun. The Moon and Earth have to be at the right "level" for the eclipse to happen.

The two types of solar eclipses are *total* and *annular*. A total eclipse occurs when the Moon is near *perigee,* the closest point of the orbit to the earth. Since the Moon is closer to the Earth at perigee, it will appear larger at that time than it will at *apogee,* the farthest point of the Moon's orbit. When the Moon appears larger to us observing it from the Earth's surface, it will cover more of the Sun than a smaller-appearing Moon at apogee. When a solar eclipse occurs at the apogee of the Moon's orbit, the eclipse will be annular—that is, it will not "cover" all the Sun. During a total eclipse, practically the entire Sun is blotted out by the Moon. It appears as though a black disk covers the Sun. During an annular eclipse, a bright halo of sunlight surrounds the black shadow disk. Annular eclipses will be visible in parts of the United States and Canada on May 30, 1984, and May 10, 1994.

The farther away the Sun is, the longer the eclipse will last. That circumstance is easy enough to understand. The farther away the Sun is, the smaller it will appear to be and the longer it will remain behind the Moon as we see it from Earth.

The Moon's shadow on the Earth is about 270 kilometers (about 170 miles) wide. It travels over the surface of the Earth at a speed of about 1,600 kilometers (1,000 miles) an hour. Therefore, there is usually very limited time to make your observations and, consequently, there is little allowance for making mistakes—for example, if you are taking pictures. The longest eclipse in recent times was on June 30, 1973. That one lasted seven minutes and fourteen seconds.

The major value of a solar eclipse is that it enables you to see parts of the Sun that you cannot ordinarily see, that is, if you have the equipment to make these observations properly and safely. Of particular interest is the *corona,* or outer atmosphere, of the Sun. It is seen to glow brightly against the darkened sky. It extends for millions of miles into space, glowing with a characteristic pearly appearance.

The *chromosphere* can also be seen when the eclipse is total. The chromosphere is a layer of solar atmosphere just above the photosphere. It is about 16,000 kilometers (10,000 miles) thick. The light it gives off is weak compared to that of the photosphere and for that reason it cannot be seen to any great extent with ordinary observation techniques. During the totality of the eclipse, the chromosphere can be made out as a rosy kind of light. You might be able to see some *prominences.* These are extensions of the chromosphere which can erupt from the solar surface and extend several hundred thousands of miles into space. The period of totality is usually not long enough to enable you to see any movement in the prominences.

The "diamond ring" effect occurs toward the end of some eclipses. There is no way to predict it. This effect is related to a phenomenon called *Baily's beads.* They are named for the English astronomer, Francis Baily (1774–1844), who first observed them in 1836. Baily's beads are irregular beads, or bands, of sunlight "peeking" around the edges of the Moon. They are caused by the Sun's light shining between mountain peaks on the Moon. They are seen just before totality and as the eclipse ends. This effect lasts for only a few seconds. When one bead seems to shine much more brightly than the others, the "diamond ring effect" is produced. Baily's beads are also seen during annular eclipses.

Sometimes bright planets, such as Jupiter and Venus, may appear just before totality. Mercury may also appear before the eclipse. However, an eclipse does not last long enough to give you much time for searching.

If you do get the chance to see a solar eclipse, work out your plan of action ahead of time. A dilemma you will face is, "Should I use my telescope to take pictures or to observe the eclipse di-

With a setup like this 4-inch equatorial refractor, you could watch a solar eclipse and take pictures at the same time. *(Courtesy Meade Instruments Corporation, Inc.)*

rectly?" This is a tough decision to make. Pictures will provide you with a permanent record, but the eclipse is best seen with the eye (protected eye, of course) on the telescope. This is not an insoluble problem. It can be solved with more equipment. You can have two or more telescopes on your mounting. While you are looking through one telescope, another can be used to take pictures. It is also possible to mount a camera on the telescope while the telescope itself is used for direct observations. Even with this kind of equipment, it is possible to get so involved with the picture-taking that you might forget to look at the eclipse.

Constellations

Constellations are groups of stars that seem to be arranged in certain patterns as we see them from Earth. Actually, the stars in a constellation are not necessarily close to each other or part of any "system." Constellations, however, provide a kind of "road map" for locating things in the heavens that you might want to look at with your telescope.

You probably know about some of these constellations, particularly the Big Dipper. The Big Dipper and the Little Dipper are unique among constellations in that each actually looks like the name it is called by. You have to really stretch your imagination to find the shapes of animals, goddesses, and so on, for which many of the constellations are named. To ancient people these shapes actually *were* gods, goddesses, animals, and heroes. For example, the Big Dipper was (and is) *Ursa Major* or "a large bear" to the ancients. To us, it is very much like a dipper and not at all like a bear, but if you think of the handle of the dipper as the bear's tail and the ladle as the body, you might be able to imagine a bear.

The stars that make up the constellations appear to stay fixed in relationship to each other. The ancients noticed there were some stars that did not stay still in relation to other stars or to each other. They seemed to wander across the heavens and, as such, were called *astered planetes,* which means "wandering stars." Today, they are called planets, and we know they are not stars but worlds that, like our own world, revolve around the Sun. Stars cannot properly be called "worlds." They are enormous balls of gases which, if anything, could be called furnaces. Any star you see out there may be a sun to planets revolving around it.

While we know that the planets revolve around the Sun, to people long ago they seemed to wander through the constellations. The apparent motion of the planets through the constellations is used today to help locate the planets. If we read in a guidebook to the stars that Saturn is in Leo at a particular time, we know approximately where to look in the sky to find Saturn. Of course, you have to know where the constellation Leo is, and there are star maps to help you locate the constellations. Astronomers, both professional and amateur, get to know the constellations better than they know the lines on their hands. There are guidebooks that give you the positions of planets in the sky so that all you have to do to find the planet is to adjust the declination and right ascension settings on your equatorial mounting (assuming you have one) according to the numbers given in the guidebook and look into your telescope. Many amateurs think it is more fun and more "proper," somehow, to locate the planet by eye, using a constellation as a guide than to depend on setting circles. It's all a matter of preference.

If you have ever looked at the stars in the night sky you know that some stars are brighter than others. When astronomers talk about the brightness of a star they use the term *magnitude.* The magnitude or brightness of a star is expressed as a number. The lower the number, the brighter the star. A few stars are so bright that they have a negative magnitude. Sirius, the brightest star in the sky, has a magnitude of -1.44. A star with a magnitude of 2 is about 2.5 times as bright as a star with a magnitude of 3. One with a magnitude of 3 is about 2.5 times as bright as one with a

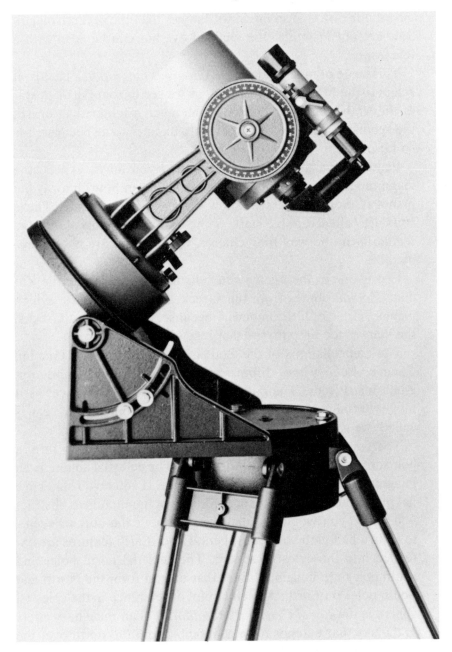

The setting circle on this 5-inch Cassegrain reflector is large and easy to read. It is on a type of equatorial mounting called a wedge. *(Courtesy Celestron International)*

magnitude of 4, and so on. Stars dimmer than the seventh magnitude are not visible to the unaided eye but can be seen with a telescope.

This scale of magnitude is the *apparent magnitude*. That is, it refers to the brightness of the star as we see it from Earth. A star of the sixth magnitude can really be much brighter than one of the second magnitude, but it appears dimmer to us because it is so far away.

Planets have magnitudes, too, but as you might expect, the magnitudes change, depending on how close or how far away the planet is. Some stars also show changes in magnitude. These stars are called variable stars. Some of these variable stars have regularity in the way they change, while others are not so predictable.

Leo is one of the twelve constellations that make up the Zodiac. *Zodiac* comes from the Greek, *Zodiakos Kyklos,* which means "circle of little animals," because, to the ancient Greeks, the stars made up patterns that resembled animal forms.

The constellations of the Zodiac are Aries, Taurus, Gemini, Cancer, Leo, Virgo, Libra, Scorpio, Sagittarius, Capricorn, Aquarius, Pisces. The path that the Sun seems to travel as it moves through the constellations over the course of a year is called the *ecliptic*.

The constellations that make up the Zodiac seem to form a belt across the sky or *celestial sphere*. The celestial sphere is an imaginary extension of the globe in space. If you could stand in a flat plain where there were no buildings or mountains to obstruct your view, you would see that the sky above the horizon seems to form a half globe or hemisphere. Other Earth features are extended into the celestial sphere. The celestial north poles and south poles are imaginary lines that extend from the North and South poles on Earth. A useful point of reference in the celestial sphere is the *Local Celestial Meridian*. It is an imaginary circle in the sky that extends from geographic south to north over the head of an observer. To cast your own Local Celestial Meridian, stand outside and face directly north. A compass will help. Another way to find north is to stand facing the North Star. Imagine a great circle running through the North Star, which is directly over you, and disappearing below the horizon, directly in back of you, which is due south. The point where the Local Celestial Meridian passes directly over you is called the *zenith.*

The Zodiac was of particular interest to the ancients, for the Sun, Moon, and planets seemed to move through the Zodiac. This is still the case today except for the planet Pluto. Pluto, however, did not matter to the ancients—it was not discovered until 1930—and it probably won't matter to you, since you won't see it unless you have an eight-inch refractor or bigger instrument. Even with the largest instruments, all you would see is a tiny, dim point of light.

Modern astronomers recognize eighty-eight constellations. Some constellations can be seen throughout the year, while others are seen only during certain seasons. Another thing involved in what constellations you see and don't see is where you live. This book is written for observers in the Northern Hemisphere. If you live in Australia, New Zealand, South Africa, or other places in the Southern Hemisphere, you won't see most of the constellations discussed in this book.

The North Circumpolar Constellations

Depending upon where you live, some constellations will always be above the horizon. That is, weather permitting, you will be able to see them any night you go out to look. You could see them in the daytime, too, were it not for the light of the Sun. They are called circumpolar because they seem to move in a "pivot" around the north celestial pole. (There are also south circumpolar constellations.) These constellations are Ursa Major (the Big Dipper or Great Bear), Ursa Minor (Little Bear or Little Dipper), Cassiopeia, Cepheus, Lynx, and Draco (the

Dragon). Just how many and how much of these constellations are visible throughout the year is dependent on where you live. If you are to the north of 40° north latitude, these constellations will always be in view. In the United States, 40° north latitude extends in a line from just south of New York City to about fifty miles south of Eureka in northwestern California. The fortieth parallel (line of latitude) extends through New Jersey, Pennsylvania, Ohio, Indiana, Illinois, Iowa, Nebraska, and Colorado-Wyoming border, Utah, Nevada, and northern California. Part of the Big Dipper is visible at 30° north latitude all year around. Most of the United States, except Hawaii, Florida, and the southern third of Texas, is north of 30° north latitude.

An important star in the Little Dipper is Polaris, or the North Star. The North Star is important to astronomers and to navigators. The North Star lies almost directly over the north celestial pole. It is the star on which you line up the polar axis of your equatorial mounting. Latitude can also be determined very simply with the North Star. At 40° north latitude, the North Star is forty degrees above the horizon. At 50° north latitude, it is fifty degrees above the horizon, and so on. At the North Pole, the North Star would be directly overhead.

The Big Dipper is used to locate the North Star. The two stars that make up the far wall of the ladle (the wall farthest away from the handle) point to the North Star.

Motions of the Stars

While the stars within a constellation remain fixed in relationship to each other, the stars as a group, however, do seem to move against the celestial sphere. The movement is an illusion caused by the motion of the Earth. There are two kinds of movement — daily motion and annual yearly motion. Daily motion is caused by the spinning of the Earth on its axis; annual motion is caused by the rotation of the Earth around the Sun. The daily motion of the circumpolar stars is what causes them to seem to "pivot" or circle around the North Star.

You can take a picture of this circling of the circumpolar stars. On a clear night set up a camera on a sturdy tripod. Point the lens directly at the North Star. Get the North Star in the middle of the picture. Open the shutter or aperture as wide as possible without blurring. Set the camera for time exposure. Leave it there for four or five hours. When you develop the picture, you will find circles of light that represent the apparent motion of the circumpolar constellations.

Noncircumpolar Constellations

These constellations rise and fall over the horizon. They also seem to "march" across the sky. Every evening, a particular constellation rises four minutes earlier than it did the evening before. Say the constellation Orion rises on the eastern horizon on a Tuesday at 9 P.M., your local time. The next day, Wednesday, it will rise on the eastern horizon at 8:56 P.M. When these constellations are not visible in the night sky, they would be visible in the daytime sky, if stars could be seen in daylight. Each evening the constellation is higher in the sky at a given time than it was the night before. Then it will be seen in the western sky each evening, eventually setting below the western horizon.

The time it takes any star to complete a complete rotation of the celestial sphere is called a *sidereal year*. Remember that the star is not really moving, so the sidereal year is actually the time it takes the Earth to move around the Sun with respect to the background of the stars. The sidereal year is 365.26 solar days. There is also a *sidereal day*. The definition of a sidereal day would seem to be obvious: It is the time it takes the Earth to rotate on its axis with respect to a fixed point, such as a star. Since the speed of the rotation of the Earth is changing, the length of a sidereal day is also changing. The average length of a sidereal day is 23 hours, 56 minutes, and 4 seconds.

The ancient peoples used the "march of the constellations" as an accurate yearly clock. As a clock, this apparent movement of the stars was far more reliable than the motions of the Moon. Lunar months do not divide equally into solar years. This circumstance causes calendars to get "out of step." Twelve lunar months are not quite a solar year, and thirteen lunar months are eighteen days more than a solar year. Various systems, such as leap years, leap months, extra months, and so on, were devised to take care of this problem. The constellations, however, were dependable. Ancient farmers knew that when Orion the Hunter was no longer visible in the night sky, it was time to start thinking about planting spring crops (Orion disappears from the night sky in early May).

Throughout the year, the constellations can be used to locate planets and other sky objects. The planets are seen to change their positions as they revolve around the Sun, but at any given time they will be found "in" a certain constellation. Of course, the planets are nowhere near the stars in that constellation, but the constellation provides a convenient backdrop for locating the planet. There are many guidebooks that give locations of planets at various times of the year. Other objects, such as galaxies (large groups of stars), star clusters, and other "deep sky" objects, can be found in constellations. For example, the M31 "Andromeda" galaxy is found in the constellation Andromeda. It is the only galaxy that can be seen with the unaided eye.

Planets

There are nine known planets—Mercury, Venus, Earth, Mars, Saturn, Jupiter, Uranus, Pluto, and Neptune. These nine planets and their satellites, comets, and everything else that

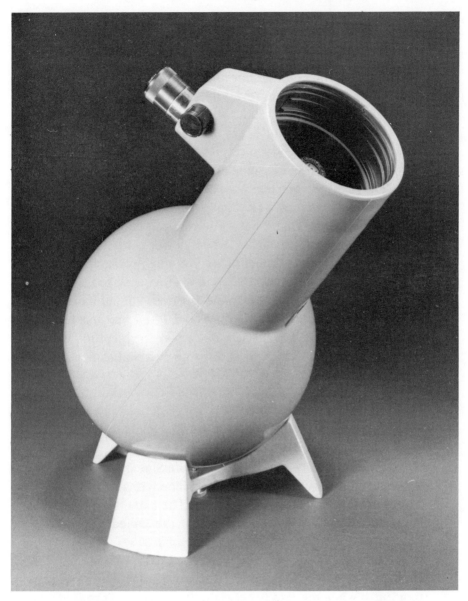

This type of instrument, called a richest-field telescope, is particularly suitable for getting wide-field views of star clusters and other sky objects. *(Courtesy Edmund Scientific Company)*

moves around the Sun make up the solar system. You may have
been a bit startled by the listing of Pluto before Neptune. Until
January 1979, Pluto was the farthest planet out from the Sun.
However, the orbits of Neptune and Pluto cross, and in January
1979, Pluto crossed inside the orbit of Neptune. In 1999, the
orbits will again cross and Pluto will once again be the most distant planet from the Sun. Many astronomers think that Pluto
may once have been a moon of Neptune.

The planets can provide some of the most rewarding and interesting observations. For the owner of a small (three-inch refractor or six-inch reflector) telescope, only four of the planets —
Venus, Mars, Jupiter, and Saturn — are close enough to always
show up as "globes," or disks, when viewed with a small telescope. Under very good conditions you might be able to get a
disk when looking at Uranus. Mercury is too close to the Sun to
show up well, and its nearness to the Sun does not put it in a very
good position for viewing. Neptune and Pluto are just too far
away. You might be able to pick out a disk for Neptune with a
four-inch refractor. Finding it at all is an accomplishment to be
proud of.

The Motions of the Planets

The planets revolve in orbits around the Sun and the direction
of the movement is counterclockwise. The paths of the planets
around the Sun are not perfect circles. The planets closer to the
Sun than Earth (Mercury and Venus) are called the inferior
planets; the others are called the *superior planets.*

When an inferior planet is between the Earth and the Sun, it is
said to be at *inferior conjunction.* Inferior planets are not visible
from Earth when the Sun is between the planet and the Earth or
— another way to say this — at *superior conjunction.* Inferior
planets appear as either "morning stars" or "evening stars."

When the Earth is between the Sun and a superior planet, the
planet is in *opposition.* When the planet moves around to the

other side of the Sun so that the Sun is between the Earth and the planet, the planet is at *conjunction.*

The *periods* of planets are important considerations when we want to know if the planets are in a favorable position for viewing. The *synodic period* of an inferior planet is the time between two inferior conjunctions. The synodic period of a superior planet is the time between two oppositions of the superior planet. The synodic period is a different amount of time than the *sidereal period* which is the amount of time it takes the planet to revolve around the Sun as measured against the background of the stars.

The farther away a superior planet is from Earth, the shorter the synodic period. The synodic period of Mars can be as much as 780 days; that of Jupiter is about 390 days. The synodic period of Pluto is about a day and a half. Mercury, an inferior planet, moves so quickly around the Sun that it has a relatively short synodic period—about 116 days. Planets are usually in the best position for observation when they are in opposition. However, the distance between the planets at opposition is also a factor in how good the viewing is. The closest distance a planet can be to Earth at opposition is called *perihelion;* the greatest distance is *aphelion.*

In September 1965, for example, Mars was 564.2 million kilometers at *aphelion* (only 35.2 million miles) from the Earth at opposition. Mars was also in aphelion in February 1980.

Sometimes the planets seem to move "backwards" in the sky. This backward, or *retrograde,* motion confused the ancients who devised all kinds of intricate systems (all wrong) to explain it. Retrograde motion is an optical illusion. It is caused by the Earth "sweeping past" the planet in its orbit. It can be compared to viewing one train from another. Suppose you are looking out of the window of a fast-moving train. The train passes a slower-moving train on the next track. As your train continues to pass the slower-moving train, the slower one will appear to be moving backward, although it is still moving forward. Retrograde motion occurs after opposition.

Observing the Planets

Following are a few suggestions for observing the planets:

Mercury

If planets have personalities, then Mercury could be described as shy. For those of us in the Northern Hemisphere, Mercury is an elusive, rather uncooperative object. It is available for observation only a few times during the year, and much of that time is daylight because, when Mercury is visible at night, it is close to the horizon and hard to see. But it is possible to observe Mercury with a telescope in daylight, particularly if the sky is a rich, deep blue.

Another problem with Mercury is that it is so close to the Sun. The closeness to the Sun makes the planet difficult to see. There is also the possibility that you could get a dangerous blast of sunlight in your telescope while you are looking into it. Even if you do manage to get Mercury in your telescopic field of view, you won't see much. A very large telescope would be needed to make out even the vaguest sort of surface features.

Space probes have revealed Mercury to be much like the Moon — pitted with craters and covered with mountains. Like the Moon, Mercury has phases as viewed from Earth. With luck and perseverance, you might be able to get a good view of Mercury, but Mercury-hunting is not for beginners. You should get experience with observing the larger superior planets (Jupiter and Saturn) before trying the possibly frustrating project of locating and observing Mercury. The farther south you live, by the way, the higher Mercury is likely to be above the horizon at favorable viewing times. This advantage holds for all the planets.

Transits of Mercury are considered to be important events by many astronomers, both professional and amateur. A transit occurs when Mercury can be seen as a tiny black spot that seems to pass across the face of the Sun. It can occur only when Mercury is at inferior conjunction. Only two more transits of Mercury will occur in this century—November 12, 1986, and November 14, 1999. If you do plan to observe a transit of Mercury, be sure to take all precautions for solar viewing or to view the transit by projection.

Venus

Next to the Sun and Moon, Venus is the brightest object in the sky. It is brightest just before and after its inferior conjunction. These periods of brightness occurring at points in the orbit are called *elongations*. Venus is frequently so bright that it can be seen in daylight, especially when the sky is a rich blue. Telescope observation in daylight is not only possible, but is often the best time. However, since Venus is close to the Sun when the Sun is above the horizon (that is, daylight), you must be careful that you do not accidentally point the telescope at the Sun while you are looking into it. Venus, at different points in its orbit, rises in the morning or evening.

Venus is covered with a thick layer of clouds. The surface of the planet is never visible. Some observers claim to have seen some markings or features in the cloud cover. If you look long enough you might see, or at least think you see, some changes in the cloud cover. Despite the lack of surface features, Venus is an interesting object to observe. Since it is an inferior planet, it shows phases, and the phases are interesting to follow. While Venus appears to be brightest when it is at elongations, only a little more than 25 percent of its surface is illuminated at that time. Through the telescope it appears as a crescent—somewhat like a crescent moon.

Following are some of the upcoming best times to observe Venus:

	Evening elongation (Western)	*Inferior Conjunction**	*Morning elongation (Eastern)*
1980	April 5	June 15	August 24
1981	November 11		
1982		January 21	April 1
1983	June 16	August 25	November 4
1984	(not a particularly good year for observing Venus)		
1985	January 22	April 3	June 13

*The days between western and eastern elongation are good times for observation, depending on weather.

Mars

Mars is a tantalizing object. It is closer to Earth than any other planet except Venus. Unlike Venus it is not covered by thick layers of clouds, and its surface is usually visible. There are a few clouds and dust storms from time to time, but much of the time the view of the planet's surface is unobstructed. The observer of Mars must be very patient. It is in the best position for observation only about every fifteen years. February 25, 1980, was one of the absolutely best days for viewing Mars. A day as good as that will not come again until 1995. However, oppositions occur about every two years. Observing is good three months before and after opposition. Therefore, good Mars-viewing is available during a six-month period about every two years. As the planet moves away from opposition and toward conjunction, it shrinks in the sky until it is no longer possible to make out a disk with a small telescope.

When viewing conditions are good, Mars appears as a reddish-yellow disk. The atmosphere makes it appear lighter at the outer parts of the disk than at the center. With a good telescope and in good local atmospheric conditions, you should be able to see the white polar caps—coverings of frozen carbon dioxide at the north and south poles. With practice you should be able to see some parts of the surface that are darker than the surrounding areas. These dark areas seem to get bigger as the polar caps melt. For years, there was speculation that these dark areas were vast growths of plant life. However, the Viking Mars Lander missions have shown Mars to be much like the Moon. It is covered with craters and some spectacular mountain peaks. The laboratory on the Viking craft failed to uncover any positive evidence of the existence of life on this neighboring planet. But the dark areas do change, both in form and color, and these changes are interesting to follow. When you observe Mars, you must be very patient. The first few times you try, you might be disappointed. One night's viewing might be not so good, but the next evening might prove to be spectacular.

Neither the Mariner spacecraft, which took pictures of Mars from orbit around the planet, nor the Viking Lander found any evidence of "canals." These canals were first reported by the Italian astronomer Giovanni Schiaparelli (1835–1910) in 1877. Schiaparelli reported that he observed thin, straight lines on the Martian surface. He called them *"canali,"* a word that means "channels" in Italian. However, the word was translated as "canals" and the misuse of this word led to speculation that "intelligent" life on Mars had built the canals to conduct water from the melting polar caps. After Schiaparelli, practically everybody who looked at Mars seemed to see the canals. Oddly enough, no one else before Schiaparelli had reported seeing these "canals." Pictures from the Mariner and Viking spacecraft have definitely disproved their existence.

The length of the Martian day is 24 hours, 37 minutes, and 23 seconds, a little longer than an Earth day. This period of rotation gives you a chance to note the changing positions of surface features. You might see changes in fifteen minutes. With patience and luck, you might be able to pick out different features at different times of the night. If you can clearly make out a particular feature, note the time it seems to be directly in front of the field of view. The next night that same feature should be in the point of the field of view thirty-seven minutes later.

To see a particular feature on Mars you need to use a fairly high magnification. However, it is still best to scan at low magnification first. Remember that high magnifications reduce the brightness of the image.

Mars has two tiny moons—Deimos and Phobos. They are only a few miles across. It is highly unlikely that you would be able to see them with a small telescope. The glare from Mars blots them out. Some observers claim to have seen them with a six-inch reflector, but that is unlikely. You would need at least a twelve-inch refractor to see them as the tiniest, vaguest points of light.

Oppositions of Mars

		(magnitude)
1980	February 25	−0.5
1982	March 31	−1.1
1984	May 11	−1.7
1986	July 10	−2.4

Jupiter

Jupiter, the largest planet in the solar system, is very "cooperative." It is easy to find and is available for observation most of the year. It is a beautiful object to observe, and it can provide many hours of sheer viewing enjoyment. Jupiter alone is worth the price of a telescope.

The outer planets—Jupiter, Saturn, Uranus, and Neptune— are built differently from the inner planets. These planets are made up mostly, or perhaps entirely, of clouds of gases (largely methane and ammonia). These gases are frozen, possibly into a kind of "slush." The Pioneer space probes have provided much new information on the nature of these planets and should provide more in the future.

The most distinctive features of Jupiter are the bands, or belts. The bands appear as reddish-brown belts against a silvery-creamy background. These bands are not permanent. They sometimes fade, and sometimes they become more intense. Astronomers have designated definite belt regions and have given them names, such as south polar region, south temperate zone, equatorial zone, north tropical zone, and so on. Nevertheless, the bands do not remain in conveniently marked-off sections. This continuous changing of the surface (actually the top of the cloud layer) is one of the fascinations of Jupiter. The Pioneer space probes revealed that Jupiter has a system of rings. However, don't expect to see them with your telescope.

Jupiter rotates on its axis fairly rapidly. However, some parts of it seem to rotate more quickly than others. The main part of the planet completes a rotation in slightly under ten hours. The parts above and below the main central part rotate a little bit faster. If you observe the planet long enough, you will be able to see this difference. You should also notice that Jupiter is a bit flattened at the poles. This flattening is evidence of the gaseous, "slushy" nature of the planet.

The Great Red Spot is one of the more interesting features of Jupiter. It is probably a huge storm in Jupiter's atmosphere. Located in the Southern Hemisphere, it is oval in shape, somewhat reddish in color. Both color and position change from time to time. Sometimes it can be seen with a small telescope and sometimes not. Seeing the Spot is reward enough for the patience and time that might be involved in looking for it.

Various disturbances, spots, and other temporary features may appear at any time. Some astronomers believe there is a pattern to the appearance of these features, but they have not been observed long enough to prove the existence of any pattern. Amateurs, more than professionals, provide most of the information on these occasional features as well as other information about Jupiter and many other planets.

There are not enough big telescopes to go around for all the professional astronomers who want to use them. When an astronomer does get some telescope time, he or she is likely to use it for some project involving deep space, rather than for study of the planets. For that reason, much of the work on planets is now done by amateurs. Many amateurs have discovered new things about planets, and you could, too.

The moons of Jupiter provide some of the most spectacular sights in the solar system. There are thirteen known moons or satellites, but only four of them can usually be seen with a telescope likely to be owned by a beginning amateur. These satellites are named Io, Europa, Ganymede, and Callisto. They are generally called the Galilean satellites because they were discovered by Galileo. They can often be seen with a pair of binoculars, and some people claim to have seen them with the eye alone. They are sixth magnitude in brightness and, if not for the glare of Jupiter, they would be visible with the naked eye. Ganymede, for example, is probably larger than the planet Mercury. The Galilean satellites revolve in almost exactly the plane of Jupiter's equator. Jupiter does not tilt on its axis very much, so the equator of this huge planet is always square on in our view. When you look at the moons of Jupiter, they always seem to be strung out in sort of a straight line. With practice, you will be able to tell one from the other. (Almanacs and "star books" give their position, but it's more fun to find them yourself.)

You can identify the different moons by their brightness and by the way they move. It does not take long to see that these satellites are definitely moving around Jupiter. Io is the closest to Jupiter and moves the fastest. Europa is dull and grayish in appearance and moves a little more slowly than Io. Ganymede is bright and brilliant. A three-inch refractor or six-inch reflector can sometimes reveal a disk. Callisto is the slowest moving of the Galilean satellites and is usually quite faint.

Sometimes the moons are eclipsed by the shadow of the huge parent planet, and sometimes the shadows of the moons can be seen moving across the face of the planet.

Oppositions of Jupiter

		(magnitude)
1980	February 24	−2.1
1981	March 26	−2.0
1982	April 25	−2.0
1983	May 27	−2.1
1984	June 29	−2.2
1985	August 4	−2.3

Saturn

Saturn is constructed in much the same way as Jupiter, and it has a system of rings. In addition to the rings, it has at least ten moons. The rings, the moons, and the markings and coloration of the planet itself make Saturn truly one of the most beautiful objects in the heavens. A small telescope, such as a three-inch refractor or even a two and a half-inch refractor, can show the rings and some of the moons. Just how well you will be able to see the rings is a matter of the angle at which Saturn seems to be tilted toward the Earth and how close to opposition Saturn is. Chances are that almost any time you observe Saturn, you will be able to see the rings. There are times when the edge of the rings directly face the Earth. Since the rings are very thin compared to their width you will not be able to see the rings at that time. However, you will get a good view of the entire disk of the planet. Fortunately, the periods during which you can't see the rings last only a few days.

The rings are 270,400 kilometers (169,000 miles) wide. They are probably no more than 16 kilometers (10 miles) thick. When conditions are right, you can see right through them to the surface of the planet. They may be the remains of a moon broken up by the enormous gravity of Saturn, or they may be particles that never came together to make a moon. Until the Pioneer spacecrafts get close enough to get a good look, no one can be quite sure of what they are made.

The ring system is composed of at least three main rings, and two fainter rings. The main rings are called A, B, and C. The division between the 16,000-kilometers (10,000 miles)-wide A ring and the B ring is called Cassini's division. It was named for the astronomer, Giovanni Cassini (1625–1712), who discovered it in 1675. Cassini's division can be seen with a small telescope. The B ring is 26,400 kilometers (16,500 miles) wide. It has a creamy color and is brighter than the A ring. The C ring, also called the crepe ring, is about 16,000 kilometers (about 10,000 miles) wide. It is difficult to pick out with a small telescope. The inner part of the C ring is about 14,400 kilometers (some 9,000 miles) from the surface of Saturn as we see it.

Bands of color can be seen on the surface of the planet (actually the top of the cloud layer). The background color is yellowish. The equatorial zone is almost white, and the polar regions are usually dark. Some observers see the polar regions as green.

Saturn is as noticeably flattened at the poles as is Jupiter, if not more so. This flattening shows that the planet is not very "solid." The weight of Saturn is actually less than the same amount of water. If you could find an ocean big enough, Saturn would float.

Of the ten known moons, perhaps four or five can be seen with a small telescope. The word "perhaps" is used because seeing the moons depends on many things, such as the positions of Earth and Saturn in their orbits when you do your observing, local Earth atmospheric conditions, the condition of your telescope, the sharpness of your eyes, and much more. The largest satellite is Titan (bigger than Mercury). It is the seventh moon out from the surface of the planet. Titan is the satellite you are most likely to be able to see (if it is not on the other side of Saturn and out of sight). Others you might see, listed in decreasing order of likelihood of sighting, are Rhea, Tethys, Dione, Hyperion, Enceladus, Mimas, Phoebe, and Iapetus. The appearance of the satellites is much the same as those of Jupiter. The moons appear to be strung out in a line.

Oppositions of Saturn
(magnitude)

1979	March 1	+0.5
1980	March 13	+0.8
1981	March 27	+0.7
1982	April 8	+0.5
1983	April 21	+0.4
1984	May 3	+0.3
1985	May 15	+0.2

Uranus, Neptune, and Pluto

Of the three outermost planets, two — Uranus and Neptune — offer the possibility of being picked up with a small telescope. Pluto is out of the question for anything smaller than an eight-inch refractor. Even the largest telescopes show it only as a tiny pinpoint of light.

The discoverer of Pluto, Clyde Tombaugh, was not a professional astronomer. However, the equipment he used was professional. He had been hired by the Lowell Observatory in Arizona to take pictures of a region of the sky in which astronomers thought a new planet might be found.

Uranus, like Saturn, and Jupiter has rings. The rings, however, were not discovered with a telescope. They were discovered, in 1977, with the help of very elaborate equipment in an airplane. For years before the discovery of the rings, astronomers had seen regular changes (which they could not explain) in the planet's magnitude. It is now known that these changes are due to the rings. You won't find the rings with your telescope. Uranus tilts sharply on its axis, so much so that it is spinning "sideways."

An equatorial mounting is almost a must for finding and observing Uranus. Adjust your setting circles according to the figures given in an ephemeris. (An ephemeris is a star almanac. It lists the positions of planets, stars, and other sky objects as they are on any particular day.) A small telescope will show Uranus as a bright bluish object. You might even be able to see a bluish-green disk if viewing conditions are very good. However, if you try to see more detail with higher powers, the image will become very dim. Over a period of observation of about ten hours, you might be able to pick up the fluctuations in brightness caused by the rings.

Uranus has five known satellites. Don't expect to find them unless you have special equipment, such as a device for "blotting out" the planet so that its glare does not hide the moons.

If you have a four-inch refractor or larger instrument, you might be able to see Neptune as a greenish disk. A smaller telescope will show a point of greenish light. As is the case with Uranus, an equatorial mounting is a near necessity for locating Neptune.

Comets

Comets, like planets, revolve around the Sun. Beyond that, however, there is little similarity between a comet and a planet. Comets are collections of gases, particles of ice, and dust. They swing around the Sun in irregular orbits. The close point of the orbit may carry the comet to within a few million miles of the Sun. The far point of the orbit may be hundreds of millions of miles beyond the orbit of Pluto. When a comet is in the right position to pick up radiation from the Sun, you might be able to see it as an airy body with a glowing "tail" of gases streaming after it. The closer it gets to the Sun, the longer and brighter the tail is likely to be.

Some comets are large enough to be seen with the eye alone, when they are relatively close to the Sun, and a few, such as Halley's Comet (which last appeared in 1910 and will appear again in 1986), can be spectacular sights in the sky. Hundreds of years ago, many people were afraid of comets, thinking their appearance was a prediction of such disasters as war and famine.

Hundreds of comets appear, disappear, and reappear with periodical regularity. These comets are listed in astronomical guidebooks. "New" comets — that is, comets that have not been discovered before — are found practically every year. Many of these comets are discovered by amateur astronomers with small telescopes. You could discover a new comet, too, and if you did it would be named after you. Having a comet named after you is one of the most exciting things that could ever happen to an amateur (or a professional) astronomer.

Hunting for new comets requires some special techniques and equipment, not to mention patience and dedication. To scan the sky for comets, you need to use low magnifications to get as wide a field of view as possible. A four-inch or six-inch refractor with a wide-angle eyepiece is used by many comet hunters.

Large, wide-field binoculars are also useful. Rich field telescopes (telescopes with short focal lengths and wide fields of view) are also popular with comet hunters. Comet hunting is not easy. Hundreds and hundreds of hours of observation are required, and there is no guarantee that you will ever find a new comet. You also need to be very familiar with the constellations and stars. You need to know if that point of light you see in your telescope or on the picture you have taken is something that has always been there or is something that has just made an appearance. Serious comet hunters take pictures of regions of the night sky in a regular pattern. Taking pictures is less tiring than looking hour after hour through a telescope, and it provides proof of the existence of the comet.

Before a comet is visible to the unaided eye (remember that not all comets can be seen without a telescope), it usually appears as a grayish blur when seen through a telescope. There are many objects that can be mistaken for comets. These include galaxies, nebulae, and star clusters.

If you do think you have found a comet, the first thing you should do is to check star maps and atlases of sky objects. If you can't find your suspected comet on a star map or in a star guide, you might have found something new, although you can't be absolutely sure at this point. The next thing you should do is to check an ephemeris to see if any comets are due at this time. If you can't find any, try to curb your excitement and look at the sky again. If what you suspect is a comet has moved in relation to the stars, you just might have seen a comet.

Remember that there are thousands of comet hunters all over the world. If you have really seen a new comet, chances are someone else has, too, so get your claim in fast. When you are fairly sure you have seen a new comet, send a telegram to the Smithsonian Observatory in Cambridge, Massachusetts. Include the following information in your telegram: the position of the suspected comet in right ascension and declination, the times you observed it at that position (date, hour, and minute), the direction the comet was moving, and as close an estimation as you can give of the apparent magnitude. Don't forget your name and address, and it is also a good idea to tell them what kind of equipment you used. Don't be afraid of making a mistake. No one is going to laugh at you. If you have not discovered a new comet, all you will have lost is the cost of the telegram, but if you are right, you just might get your name in all the astronomy books (not to mention the newspapers) as the discoverer of a new comet.

It would be very frustrating to really discover a new comet only to find that someone else found it and reported it a few minutes before you did. But you will have the satisfaction of a reply from the observatory acknowledging that you were one of the first people to find the new comet.

Asteroids

Between the orbit of Mars and Jupiter, there are thousands of chunks of rock revolving around the Sun. These chunks are

called *asteroids*. They are also called minor planets, or plane-
toids. Probably the remains of a planet that broke apart, they
range in size from tiny dust particles to "minor planets" 1,000
kilometers (600 miles) in diameter. Some, if you know where to
look, can be seen with the unaided eye. Many of them enter the
Earth's atmosphere and are seen as meteors streaking through
the sky. If the entire meteor does not burn up in the atmosphere,
portions of it might land on the Earth. These pieces are called
meteorites. A number of them can be seen with a small telescope. An equatorial mounting and an ephemeris are essential to
finding asteroids; they appear as tiny points of light. It is interesting to follow their movements over a period of days or weeks.

Beyond the Solar System

Don't think your observations need to be limited to the Moon,
Sun, and planets. A telescope as small as a two-and-a-half-inch
refractor will reveal many wonderful and beautiful sky objects to
you. Remember, there are many millions of stars that you can't
see with your eye alone. Scanning the heavens with a low-
power, wide-angle eyepiece will reveal a richness of stars you
never dreamed was there.

Stars

The Sun is only one of about 100 trillion stars in our galaxy or
star group. Only about 6,000 of these stars (about 3,000 per
hemisphere) are visible to the unaided eye, and not all of those
can be seen at the same time. The smallest telescope will reveal
many more stars, and a larger telescope with good light-gathering power will reveal millions and millions of stars.

Of particular interest to amateurs are the so-called "double
stars." A double star is a group of two or more stars that seem to

lie very close together as we see them from Earth. To the unaided eye, the double star appears as one point of light. The telescope, depending on its size and quality, should "separate" one point of light into two or more points of light. As mentioned in the discussion on buying a telescope, the resolving power, or ability of a telescope to separate two points of light, is a very important consideration in deciding what telescope to buy. You will recall that the resolving ability of a telescope is expressed in terms of seconds of an arc.

Some double stars are *binary stars*. In a binary star system, the two stars revolve around each other. Over the years, the telescopic appearance of the system will change.

A double star is particularly interesting if the members are of sharply different magnitudes or color. The color of a star is an indication of its heat. White stars with a little bit of blue or green in them are the hottest — about 25,000° C (about 45,000° F). Pure white stars have a temperature of about 11,000° C (about 19,800° F). Yellow stars (including our Sun) have a temperature of about 6,000° C (about 12,800° F), and orange or red stars are the coolest, with temperatures in the 2,600° C range (about 4,700° F). These colors are not very obvious. A bit of practice is needed to pick up the subtle differences in color between a white star and yellow star, for example. The difference, however, is more obvious if two stars of different colors are seen close together in a double star. In some double star systems the difference is quite striking.

The Milky Way

Our galaxy is called the Milky Way galaxy. That name comes from the whitish appearance of the part of the galaxy we can see. On almost any clear night, you can see a hazy circle of light extending over the entire celestial sphere. That circle of hazy light is generally called the Milky Way. It is one "arm" of our galaxy.

The Milky Way galaxy is constructed like a giant pinwheel. There is a central core or disk from which "arms" extend. Our Sun lies in one of these arms and what we see as the "Milky Way" are millions of stars in the arm. A small telescope can resolve the hazy light into the tiny points of light which are really stars.

Star Clusters

Among the more beautiful objects in the galaxy are groups of stars called *star clusters*. There are two main types — *open clusters* and *globular clusters*. Both types can be seen with a small telescope, but larger instruments, such as eight-inch and larger refractors, are better for viewing globular clusters. Open clusters are quite spectacular. They are the jewelry of the sky, appearing like diamonds against a black background. As the name suggests, open clusters are loose collections of stars. Most are seen in the Milky Way region. The *Pleiades* (also called the Seven Sisters) and the *Hyades* are among the more frequently observed open clusters.

Globular clusters are incredibly huge balls of stars. Hundreds of thousands of stars can be in one globular cluster. These clusters appear spectacular enough in photographs taken with large telescopes, but they are not too impressive as viewed through a small telescope. With a small telescope, a globular cluster looks like a hazy, blurred sphere. You may be able to pick out a few individual stars at the edge of the cluster.

Nebulae

Nebulae (plural; one is "nebula") are clouds of gas and dust in our own galaxy. Sometimes the word "nebula" is used to describe a galaxy, but that is not a correct use of the word. The confusion comes from the old days when astronomers did not know that galaxies were systems of stars separate and very far away from our own star system. Some nebulae and some galaxies look alike when viewed through a telescope, but in reality they are very different.

Nebulae come in all sizes, shapes, and degrees of brightness and darkness. Some, called *planetary nebulae,* show up as small, faint disks. *Dark nebulae* give off no light. The nebula of greatest interest to the owner of a small telescope is the Great Nebula in Orion. It can be seen with the unaided eye, and it shows up as an interesting glow in a small telescope.

Galaxies

There are billions of galaxies in the universe, each one containing billions of stars. Large telescopes, such as the 200-inch reflector at Mount Palomar, have photographed thousands of galaxies. There are three basic types of galaxies: spiral, elliptical, and irregular. The names describe the general shape of the galaxy. Our own galaxy is a spiral. A typical spiral galaxy has a central area or nucleus with "arms" extending in a spiral pattern out from the nucleus. The stars and gas clouds rotate around the nucleus. Elliptical galaxies have no arms and are shaped somewhat like a flat egg. Irregular galaxies have no particular pattern in their structure. In the Southern Hemisphere, two neighboring irregular galaxies, the *Magellanic Clouds,* can be seen with the unaided eye and are popular objects with amateur astronomers. A few galaxies are within the range of small telescopes. One of these is the *Andromeda* galaxy, an elliptical galaxy some two million light-years away.

Names of Sky Objects

Names of stars, nebulae, clusters, galaxies, and so on can be confusing. The confusion comes from the use of many different naming systems. One of the earliest star-naming systems was set up by the German astronomer Johann Bayer (1572–1625) in 1603. In this system, the stars in a constellation are assigned a Greek letter followed by the Latinized name of the constellation. The brightest star is designated "alpha," the next "beta," and so on through the Greek alphabet. For example, according to this system, the brightest star in the constellation Scorpio would be Alpha Scorpius.

There are only twenty-four letters in the Greek alphabet, and there are many constellations with more than twenty-four stars to be named. Awareness of this rather obvious fact encouraged the British astronomer John Flamsteed (1646–1719) to propose a new system. His star catalogue *Historia Coelestis Britannica* was published posthumously in 1725. He named the stars in a constellation by number. The numbers are determined by the right ascension of the star, starting at the western end of the constellation. Bayer's system, however, is generally preferred. Of course, Bayer's system cannot be used for stars twenty-fifth in magnitude and beyond in constellations. Stars also have their "own" names, such as Sirius, Altair, and Mizar. The possibility that a sky object can be referred to by more than one system adds to the confusion.

You will also come across letters such as NGC, M, O, Σ (Greek letters omicron and sigma), H, h, and many more. These letters refer to catalogues that were developed over the years by astronomers and international conferences of astronomers. The letter M, for example, refers to Charles Messier (1730–1817). He put together a list of his many discoveries. For example, M31 is the thirty-first object listed in Messier's catalogue. M31 is also known as the Andromeda galaxy. NGC is an abbreviation for *New General Catalogue,* a list of nebulae and clusters first published in 1888. The NGC now also includes galaxies.

Naming systems for double stars are particularly confusing. They are listed by at least ten different systems. The Greek letter beta (β) is used in the double star naming system developed by the American astronomer Sherburne Wesley Burnham

(1838–1921) in 1910. This was an unfortunate choice, since there is confusion with the Bayer star naming system. The capital Greek letter sigma (Σ) refers to the naming system set up by Friedrich Georg Wilhelm von Struve (1793–1864), a German astronomer. More confusion has been provided by the fact that his son, Otto Wilhelm von Struve (1819–1905), also catalogued double stars. His listings are designated by either OΣ or O$\Sigma\Sigma$. The von Struves were not the only father-and-son team in the double star listing business. There was the great British astronomer, Sir William Herschel (1738–1822); his double stars are preceded by an H. His son, Sir John Herschel (1792–1871), continued the family tradition, and a double star preceded by an "h" comes from his catalogue. Later, John Herschel "recatalogued" some of his father's listings. These are designated "Hh." As if there was not enough confusion about naming stars, two more double star cataloguers had names starting with "H." These were George Washington Hough (1836–1909) and T. J. Hussey. Their double stars are designated "Ho" and "Hu" respectively.

This discussion of how sky objects are named is intended to prepare you for the following listing of some of the more interesting stars, nebulae, clusters, et cetera, you might care to look at. These objects are listed by month and constellation. The months are those in which the listed constellations are near the local celestial meridian in the Northern Hemisphere, particularly in the middle latitudes of the United States and Canada. The listing of a constellation as a "March observation" does not mean that March is the only month in which the objects in the constellation can be seen. It does mean that the constellation is high in the sky at night during March and is therefore in a good position for observation. Actually, all or part of the constellation would still be in the night sky at least two months before and two months after the designated month.

The objects selected for this listing are particularly suitable for viewing with a small telescope. This list is only a small sampling of the many objects there are to be seen with a small telescope. The names given for the objects are the ones in most general use.

JANUARY

Perseus   An interesting part of the Milky Way containing some very rewarding objects for small telescopes is found in this constellation. One of the most outstanding features in this constellation is the Double Cluster H.VI.33 and H.VI.34 (or NGC 869 and NGC 864). It is visible to the unaided eye as a concentration of light. Through a telescope, such as a three-inch refractor or six-inch reflector, it is seen as two open star clusters. These clusters, with dimmer stars in the background, are a dazzling display. Few telescopes have a wide enough field of view to see them both in the field at once.

Other objects in Perseus *include:*

Beta (β) Persei (or Algol), a variable double star that varies from 2.2 magnitude to 3.5 magnitude in a pattern that repeats every two days, twenty hours, and forty-six minutes. It is a type of star called an *eclipsing binary,* in which one star in the pair eclipses the other.

Double star Eta (η) Persei. One is yellow and the dimmer star is quite blue.

Taurus (The Bull)   In this constellation of the Zodiac, you will find the Pleiades, or Seven Sisters. Seven stars are visible in this cluster to most unaided eyes. A small telescope will reveal hundreds of stars. One of the giant telescopes, such as the Hale, can take a picture showing thousands of stars. The beauty of the cluster is increased by the thin nebula that is "lit up" by the stars in the cluster. Alcyone, a star toward the center, is a quadruple star.

Hyades, another open cluster.

Aldebaran, the bright red star that is the "eye" of the bull. It has a 11.2-magnitude red companion. Finding it with a three-inch reflector is a test of telescope and observer.

Σ730, double star, yellowish and bluish.

FEBRUARY

Orion (The Hunter)   The king of the night sky in the winter is Orion. High in the sky in February at "prime time," it also dominates the sky from December to April. Viewers in the Southern Hemisphere can also see this constellation. In Orion is one of the most magnificent sights in the sky—the Great Nebula (NGC 1976, M42). Through a small telescope it is seen as a green veil surrounding the multiple star Theta (θ). The veil is seen to have many twists and "ruffles" varying in intensity of light. You may well find that you will spend hours gazing at this magnificent show in the sky.

Other objects in Orion:
    Σ627, a double star with interesting, difficult-to-name colors.
    Lambda (λ), a double star, yellow and gray.
    Rigel (at the foot), double star, yellowish-white and orange.
    Theta, mentioned above, is a quadruple star. The four stars form the general outline of a baseball diamond. They are often called the Trapezium.
    Σ747, double star, white and blue.

Auriga (The Charioteer)   The Milky Way passes through this constellation. Three good clusters can be seen here. These are M36, M37, and M38. M38 is the favorite of many amateurs. It is seen in the shape of a cross with a pair of bright stars in each arm.

MARCH

Gemini (The Twins) This is the featured constellation as winter turns to spring. The major attraction is the open cluster

M35. Covering a wide area of sky, it cannot be seen all at once. The double star Pollux, one of the Twins' "heads," is the brightest binary pair visible from the Northern Hemisphere. Both members of the pair are yellow. They are just beginning to open up. The widest separation will be reached in about seventy-five years. Other features: a bright nebula, H.IV.45; Kappa (κ), a double star, deep yellow and pale blue.

Castor, the other "head" may be composed of as many as six stars. There is a binary and a third star rotating around the binary. Each of these may be a double.

Canis Major (The Greater Dog)   This group includes Sirius, the brightest star, which is a quadruple. The M41 open cluster has some beautiful orange stars.

APRIL

Leo (The Lion)   The bright star Regulus has an apparent dim partner. Regulus may not be a true double. The partner may appear to be a double of Regulus because of the way we see it from Earth. This constellation has a number of interesting double stars including Gamma (γ), the beautiful gold-and-greenish binary.

MAY

Bootes (The Herdsman)   The major star in this constellation, Arcturus, is the third brightest. There are a number of good doubles including Σ1785, a yellow-and-blue binary.

JUNE

Virgo (The Virgin)   Highlighted by the bright star Spica, this constellation holds a number of nebulae you might be able to pick out on good viewing nights. These include M84 and M86 which can be seen in the same field of view. M84 is just a little brighter than M86. M59 is another interesting nebula, and you might be able to make out many other faint nebulae in the region of M59.

JULY

Scorpio (The Scorpion)   The bright red star Antares leads this group. It is a double, but you will probably need at least a four-inch refractor to make out the greenish partner. Scorpio contains some worthwhile open clusters, including M6, which many observers consider to be one of the most beautiful. It is shaped somewhat like a flower, with bright stars forming the flower outline. And Σ6281 is a cluster shaped like a trapezoid. This constellation also contains many globular clusters.

Corona Borealis (The Northern Crown)   This constellation has an interesting variable star. It is usually sixth magnitude, but sometimes it fades to about fourteenth magnitude. There is no known pattern to these changes, and no one knows what causes them. You might find it interesting to take a look at it once in a while to see what is going on.

AUGUST

Hercules   This dim constellation is not particularly easy to find. Once you do find it, you will be rewarded with one of the few globular clusters worth the time of a small telescope owner. M13 is the largest, brightest globular cluster visible from the Northern Hemisphere. Sometimes you might be able to pick out individual stars at the edges. If you own a large telescope (eight inches or more), it is a grand sight, indeed. Hercules also offers many fine double stars, and some other globular clusters not as good for small telescopes as M13.

SEPTEMBER

Lyra (The Lyre)   contains one of the more fascinating sky objects—the "ring" nebula or, more officially, M57. It is a type of nebula called *annular planetary*. It is bright, bluish in color, and its smoke-ring shape accounts for its name. It can be seen with a three-inch refractor but bigger telescopes are needed to really pick out the ring shape. The brightest star in the constellation is Vega. It has a faint, orange companion. The double star Zeta (ζ) is good for small telescopes; the two stars are white and cream.

Cygnus (The Swan)   This is one of the most rewarding areas of the sky for a small telescope owner. It lies in the Milky Way and is filled with clusters, double stars, and triple stars. This constellation is also called the Northern Cross. The Beta star (β), a beautiful yellow and deep blue pair, is a good double for a small telescope; Σ2578 is a pretty, white and pale blue pair. There are a number of faint, but very extensive, nebulae that are rewarding to observe with low power, wide fields. M39 is a triangular cluster, best observed at low power. For this one you might discover that the finder gives best results. Try it with binoculars. Another fine cluster is Σ7039. The patterns of light in Cygnus change, and the entire field seems to be "sprinkled" with many points of light.

Aquila (The Eagle)   This group is highlighted by the bright star Altair. Altair, Vega, and Deneb make up one of the most distinctive features of the late summer sky — the "summer triangle." The constellation contains a number of interesting, if unspectacular, double stars; Σ2404 is a pretty yellow and blue pair.

OCTOBER

Pegasus   The great Square of Pegasus is the most distinctive feature of the late summer and early autumn sky. The main feature of interest for small telescope work is M15, a large globular cluster. A small telescope will show it as a cloudy object with a blazingly bright center. The Beta (β) star is an interesting irregular. It shows a period of sorts that runs about thirty-five days.

NOVEMBER

Andromeda   The object of most interest in this constellation is the only galaxy that can be seen with the unaided eye, and one of the few that can really be observed with a small telescope. This is the famous Andromeda galaxy, M31. It is a relative "neighbor" as galaxies go—only 2,200 million light-years away. A small telescope shows it as an elliptical object, with a bright center surrounded by a haze. The two nearby "satellite" galaxies are beyond the reach of small telescopes. Also of interest are H.VII.32, an open cluster, and Σ3050, a yellow binary system that is closing up.

DECEMBER

Cetus (The Whale)   Mira is an interesting variable star that many amateur astronomers have studied. It varies from magnitude 2 to about magnitude 10 over an approximately 330-day period. There is a spiral galaxy, M77. You might get a hazy view of it on good viewing nights.

ALL YEAR

Circumpolar constellations

Ursa Major (The Great Bear or The Big Dipper)   Two galaxies, M81 and M82, can often be picked up in the same field of view at low powers. You won't see much detail, but they are bright, and you should be able to pick them out as points of light. M82 might be seen as a curved streak of light. Mizar, the second star in the handle, is a double; both partners are greenish white. Without a telescope you can see another partner, Alcor. Another star lies between Alcor and Mizar. The Xi (ξ) star is the first binary for which the period (sixty years) was worked out. It is now at a point of very wide separation. M97, the "owl nebula," is a good object for a small telescope at low power. It is a large, rather dim planetary nebula.

Cepheus There are no clusters here, but there are some interesting doubles and variables, including Herschel's "garnet star," so named because it looks like a big red piece of jewelry. It is an irregular variable (magnitude 3.7 to 4.7) with an approximate period of five to six years. Σ2816 is a triple, a yellowish star in the middle with a blue star on either side. The Delta (δ) star is a yellow-and-blue double. The bright star in the pair is a variable (3.8–4.6) with a period of 5.3 days.

Cassiopeia This constellation looks like an M or W, depending upon where it is in its pivot around the North Star. It lies in a rich part of the Milky Way. There are some rewarding clusters, including M52, a beautiful group, somewhat triangular in shape; H.VIII.78, a group of ninth-magnitude stars shaped like a mushroom; and H.VI.30, a rather faint but large compressed cluster. There are also a good many doubles, including the yellow and purple Eta (η) star, and Σ163, rich gold and blue with good contrast.

Ursa Minor (The Little Bear or The Little Dipper) This is a distinctive constellation if for no other reason than its inclusion of Polaris, the North Star. Polaris is the Alpha (α) star of the group. It is a double star, white and blue. You should be able to separate it with a three-inch refractor or six-inch reflector.

Using Your Microscope

What is there to see with a microscope? Just about everything. There is hardly anything in this world that cannot be examined at least a little bit more closely with a microscope. In a way, there is much more to see on our own planet with a microscope than there is to see in the skies with a telescope. While there are billions of stars in our own and other galaxies, only several thousand of them are available to you with a small telescope. There seems to be no limit, however, to things to look at with a microscope.

Of course, some materials need a little more preparation than others before they can be observed with a microscope. For example, if you just put a potato on the stage of your microscope, you will see absolutely nothing but blackness. But if you cut a very thin slice of potato and carefully put it on a slide, what you will see will be fascinating and beautiful and will tell you a great deal about how potatoes are put together.

Since there is practically no limit to what you can see with a microscope, the following is only a sampling of some of the many fascinating, wonderful things there are to view.

A Few Hints on Using a Microscope

First of all, treat your microscope with respect. Keep it in a case, or at least covered, when you are not using it. When you put it on a desk or table, do so gently. Knocking the microscope against something could put the lenses out of adjustment.

When you focus the microscope, move the tube only in an upward direction while you are looking into it. Start with the objective close to the slide. Move the tube downward only while you are looking at the microscope from the side. Then, while looking into the microscope, move the tube up until the image comes into focus. Focusing in this way will avoid damage to slide and objective from accidentally jamming the objective into a slide. If the focusing mechanism on your microscope moves the stage rather than the tube, avoid moving the stage up toward the objective while looking into the microscope.

Your first tendency will be to use your microscope with one eye closed. You should, however, try to keep both eyes open. This will be difficult at first, but eventually will result in less eye strain and more viewing comfort. At first, put a hand over the eye that is not over the eyepiece.

Clean the lenses with a fine camel's-hair brush. Never use ordinary tissues. You can use lens tissue, but use it carefully, rubbing lightly in a circular direction.

You might want to try taking pictures with your microscope. Most manufacturers make expensive, elaborate models equipped with everything that is needed for microphotography. However, almost any good camera can be attached to a microscope. Many camera manufacturers sell adapter sleeves specifically designed for use with their cameras. Be prepared to do an awful lot of experimenting to find the best combination of light, exposure times, diaphragm settings and so on.

Looking at Yourself

You don't have to look any farther than yourself to find something interesting to observe. Try looking at a strand of your hair. It may take a bit of manipulating to get the hair in your field of view. Hair has a tendency to be springy. Put the slide on the stage and then place the hair on the slide. Hold down the hair with the stage clips (if your microscope has them). You may be

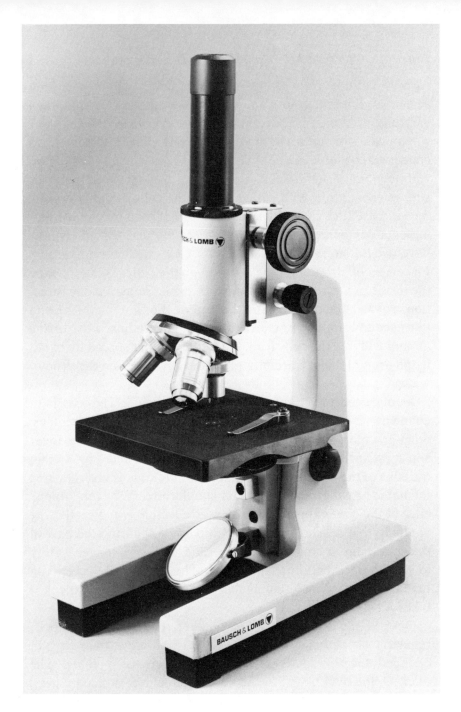

This microscope is suitable for both home and school use. *(Courtesy Bausch and Lomb)*

surprised at how transparent a strand of hair is. If you can, look at hair of different colors and thicknesses. Focus up and down carefully with the fine adjustment to get different views.

You can also see some of your own cells. The easiest cells to collect and observe are cells from the inside of your cheek. You will need some toothpicks, a medicine dropper, a slide, cover slip, and something with which to stain the cells. Iodine solution, the kind used for cuts, will do. Iodine is not used much for treating cuts anymore, but most drugstores still carry it. You may have used a similar material in school called Lugol's Solution. Place a *small* drop of iodine solution on the slide. Gently scrape the inside of your cheek with the toothpick. Scrape in one direction, not back and forth. Stir the end of the toothpick (the end you used to scrape your cheek) around in the iodine. The stirring around will free the cells from the toothpick and spread them out in the drop of stain. Carefully place the cover slip on the drop of water.

A suggested way to place cover slip on liquid: The idea is to eliminate air bubbles as much as possible. To avoid air bubbles, don't just plop the cover slip on the liquid. First, place the cover slip at an angle to the drop of liquid just to one side of it so that the edge of the cover slip in contact with the slide is just touching the liquid. At the same time, you should be holding the "open" edge of the cover slip with a long needle, a thin wooden stick, or anything that will hold the cover slip up. Anchoring the part of the cover slip in contact with the slide with your finger, gently lower the open end onto the liquid. The liquid will "creep" up the cover slip, eliminating air bubbles. As you might expect, it takes a bit of practice.

Observe the cells first with low power. The cells appear as irregularly shaped flat objects. Try to find some that are not clumped together and that don't have too many folds. The nucleus, the oval object in the center, should be stained a deep brown. The rest of the cell will be more lightly stained. Many tiny objects will be seen sprinkled throughout the cell.

More of Yourself. Fingernail clippings: Clip as thin as possible. Do not use a cover slip.

Flaked-off dead skin from your scalp and other areas: It's not all dandrull, although some of it might be.

Dirt from under your fingernails: Looking at it with a microscope is a good way to encourage you to keep your fingernails clean.

Water

Within a drop of water can be found some of the most fascinating, and often incredible, things you can expect to see anywhere. However, we are not talking about just any old drop of water. For example, one would hope that a drop of drinking water from the tap would contain nothing that wiggles, squirms, or swims. Of course, drinking water is examined all the time by public health officials to check for those and other sorts of things. You might want to check your drinking water yourself from time to time. If you do see a lot of stuff suspended in the water, or things that wiggle, squirm, and swim, tell the water company.

The most rewarding water, as far as microscopic observation is concerned, is pond water. Collecting pond water is easy. Just take a jar down to the pond and pick up some water. After you collect the water, take a look at the jar with the unaided eyes. You will probably see little things swimming around. Some of them might be big enough for you to make out the shape, and from time to time you will pick up fairly large organisms, such as insects, worms, snails, fish, and more.

To observe the pond water in a microscope, put a small drop of it on a slide, cover with a cover slip, and look. Some of the larger living things in the water might be crushed by the cover slip. There are a number of ways to accommodate these larger specimens. One way is to use a *depression slide*. This is a slide with a little indentation in it. An interesting way to use this kind of slide is to make a *hanging drop* slide. First, lightly smear a cover slip with petroleum jelly. Then place the drop of water on the cover slip. Carefully turn the cover slip over and place it over the depression. The little creatures will now have swimming room. Of course, you can expect to spill quite a few drops of water before you get the technique just right. A disadvantage of the hanging drop is that it tends to vibrate and shake around.

You can use the petroleum jelly to make your own depression slide. Make a circular well on the slide with the jelly. The walls of the well should be no more than one or two millimeters high. You can make a hanging drop as before. You probably won't be able to use the highest powers with this arrangement, but any animal big enough to need this kind of preparation is best seen at lower powers.

Most of the tiny living things you will see in pond water are completely or partially transparent. Careful focusing will enable you to see many of the internal parts of these creatures. Since light passes right through them, it is sometimes best to cut down the light a little. Bright light is usually not very good for seeing the internal detail of these organisms. Experiment with different light levels to find which is the best.

Another problem you will encounter is the apparently rapid movement of many of these organisms. Actually, they are moving quite slowly, but your microscope magnifies their speed as well as their size. They might seem to zip across your field of view at the speed of a racing car. The width of your field of view varies with the magnification and the kind of eyepiece you use. However, suppose that your field of view is two millimeters across. If one of the creatures takes half a second to cross the field of view, it is moving at the rate of four millimeters a second, which translates roughly into about forty-eight feet an hour, or about .009 miles an hour.

Slowing them down: A little bit of a thick, transparent liquid called methyl cellulose added to the water will slow down the animals. If you can't get any of that, put a few individual strands of absorbent cotton in the water. The strands will act as barriers, slowing down the animals so you can get a better look at them.

How big are these organisms? It is not very convenient to measure one of these tiny living things with a ruler. However, you can get a pretty good idea of their size if you know the diameter of the field of view. Some microscope manufacturers give you this information either in the instruction book or stamped on the eyepiece or objective. If not, you can figure it out for yourself. The easiest way is to put a transparent metric ruler over the light hole on the stage of your microscope. Focus, and move the ruler around until the measurement lines are directly across the center of the field of view. You can then directly read the ruler. Do the same for all the powers of your microscope. If you can't find a transparent metric ruler, you can make one yourself. With a very fine-line pen, mark off a few millimeter rulings on a flat piece of clear plastic. Put that on your microscope and measure the field of view as described before.

Suppose your field of view is one millimeter across. You will recall that one millimeter is equal to 1,000 microns. So, if one of the creatures seems to be about half as long as the field of view, it is about 500 microns long.

"Intensifying" the water: You can increase the number and kinds of creatures in your pond-water sample by making a hay infusion. Start off with a jar as you did before. Put some hay or grass in the jar. You could also throw in a few dried leaves. Cover this material with pond water. (Leave the jar uncovered.) Put the unlidded jar of water in a cool (60°–70° F; 16°–20° C) place with moderate light. Let it stand two or three days. A hay infusion smells pretty awful after a few days, so be sure to keep it where it is not likely to bother anybody. For instance, no one will appreciate a hay infusion in the living room.

After a few days, examine drops of water from your hay infusion. Try water from different areas of the jar—the top, middle, sides, bottom, surfaces of leaves, stalks of hay, and so on. You should find that different kinds of creatures will be

A microscopic view of bird feathers. *(Courtesy Bausch and Lomb)*

found in different areas. Another thing you will notice is that the types of organisms will change with the passage of time. The first couple of days when you look at the water, one or two types of living things will seem to be the most numerous. After a few more days, a different type of organism will be most prevalent. The hay infusion will not last forever. After a while, you will see fewer and fewer things. The final stage is usually dominated by bacteria too small for you to see well without a research-quality microscope and without special staining methods. Of course, you won't know the names of all the living things you will see, but you will begin to recognize some of them. You can give them your own names, like "Charleys" or "Judys." Be sure to wash your hands thoroughly after working with a hay infusion.

You will see thousands of different kinds of living things. Some of them will be animals, some plants, and some that are like both animals and plants. Generally, animals move and plants do not, but there are many exceptions to this generality, especially among the creatures you will see in your water samples. Some organisms that can be regarded as plants, such as some kinds of *algae,* move through the water.

Many biologists prefer to call one-celled organisms *protists* rather than animals or plants. The animal-like protists are the *Protozoa,* and you will see a lot of those in a hay infusion. Some Protozoa move through the water fairly quickly, moving themselves with little hairlike projections. Others seem to crawl along. You can't begin to identify them all, but some of the books listed in the Resources chapter can help. Following are some of the classes of Protozoa you might see:

Ciliates [SILL-ee-ates]: These move with tiny hairlike projections called cilia [SILL-ee-uh]. They act somewhat like oars. Some ciliates are covered all over with cilia. Others have the cilia concentrated in certain parts of the cell. Some move smoothly through the water, while others move in a jerky or bouncing fashion. *Paramecia* [PARE-uh-MEE-see-uh] are well-known members of this group. You may see those, but you are

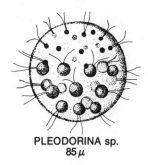

PLEODORINA sp.
85 μ

PHACUS sp.
100 μ

SPHAERELLA sp.
100 μ

CRYPTOGLENA sp.
100 μ

EUGLENA sp.
100 μ

A group of typical flagellates. *(Courtesy Xerox Education Publications, Columbus, Ohio)*

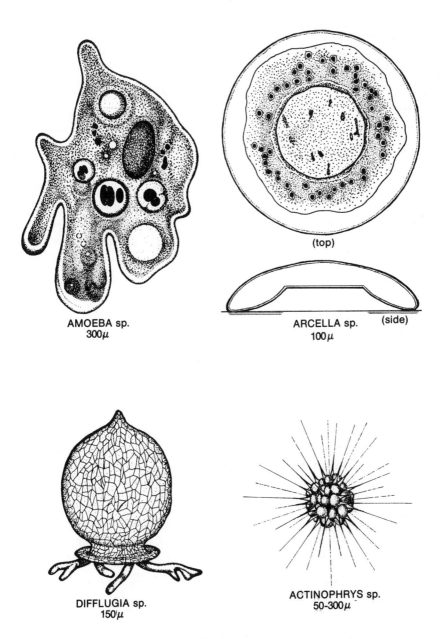

AMOEBA sp.
300μ

ARCELLA sp.
100μ

(top)

(side)

DIFFLUGIA sp.
150μ

ACTINOPHRYS sp.
50-300μ

A group of typical sarcodines. *(Courtesy Xerox Education Publications)*

more likely to see *Colpidia* [kole-PID-ee-uh]. These are smaller than paramecia.

Flagellates [FLADGE-uh-lates] have one or two whiplike "rudders" that move them through the water. One of these whiplike things is called a flagelleum [fla-JELL-ee-um]. You will probably see many of these flagellates, but many are so small they will seem like little blurs zipping across your field of view.

Sarcodina [sahr-koh-DEE-nah]: These move by changing the shape of the cell and sort of creeping along. Among this group is the *amoeba* [ah-MEE-bah], perhaps the best known of the more infrequently seen protists. Some seem to "crawl"; they are likely to be found along the bottom of the jar, the sides, or on the surface of leaves and hay sprigs. The "creeping" of an amoeba slows the movement of **protoplasm,** the material that is the living part of all cells. Some sarcodina have shells. A fairly common, shelled type is called *Arcella* [ar-SELL-ah]. They have yellowish shells and look like "golden doughnuts."

Plantlike protists: These are the *algae* [AL-jee]. You are more likely to see these in freshly collected pond water than in a several-days-old hay infusion. The conditions in a hay infusion tend to kill algae after a while. Some algae are "loners"—single cells—, while others occur in long chains of cells or balls of cells. If the algae are alive, the green color will give you a clue that they are algae. Algae are plantlike because they have chlorophyll and make food through photosynthesis. In some kinds of algae the chlorophyll is arranged in beautiful spiral and twisted patterns. One of the more common types of algae is *Spirogyra* [SPY-row-JIE-ruh]. In the summer you can sometimes find thick mats of spirogyra growing on the surface water of ponds. Take some of this home in a jar. Pick up a few strands with a pair of tweezers and place them in water on the slide. Spirogyra's chlorophyll looks like a green, twisted ribbon.

Euglena [you-GLEE-nuh] is an example of an organism that can be thought of as an alga or flagellate. It is a one-celled organism and has a flagelleum. Its cholorophyll gives it a beautiful

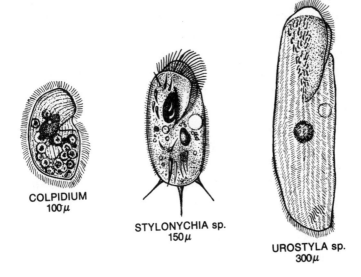

COLPIDIUM
100μ

STYLONYCHIA sp.
150μ

UROSTYLA sp.
300μ

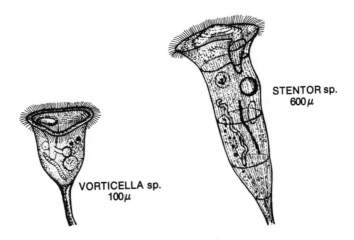

STENTOR sp.
600μ

VORTICELLA sp.
100μ

A group of typical ciliates. *(Courtesy Xerox Education Publications)*

green color. It has a red, light-sensitive "eyespot" at the base of the flagelleum. Sometimes there can be so many Euglena that the water is colored a bright green. Since Euglena has chlorophyll, it can be thought of as a plantlike protist—that is, an alga. However, since it actively moves about and since sometimes eats instead of making its own food, it can also be thought of as an animal-like protist.

Many-celled animals in your water sample: Just because you need a microscope to see a creature does not necessarily mean it is only one cell. There are also quite a few that can just barely be seen with the naked eye. Following is a survey of some of the kinds of many-celled animals you might see in your water samples.

Rotifers: These are very interesting creatures and are quite likely to be included in the population of your hay infusion. They come in many shapes and sizes. They generally creep along by expanding and contracting their bodies. Some move by means of rotating circles of cilia that are rather like "outboard motors." These circles of cilia are also used to take in food, and they are the reason these creatures are sometimes called "wheel animals." They are transparent enough for you to see many of the internal organs.

Worms: There are many different kinds of animals that can be described as "worms." We think of a worm as something that is longish and somewhat cylinder-shaped and moves along by squirming or creeping. Actually, "worms" can be quite different kinds of animals. The kinds of worm you are most likely to see in your water sample or hay infusion are those that are called nematodes [NEE-muh-toads]. These are usually white or clear, tapered at the ends, and they move in a whipping, side-to-side motion. The first time you see one, you might be quite startled when this large organism (compared to most one-celled creatures you will see) comes whipping through your field of view.

Other kinds of worms you might see will have many bristles and projections on them. These worms are related to earth-

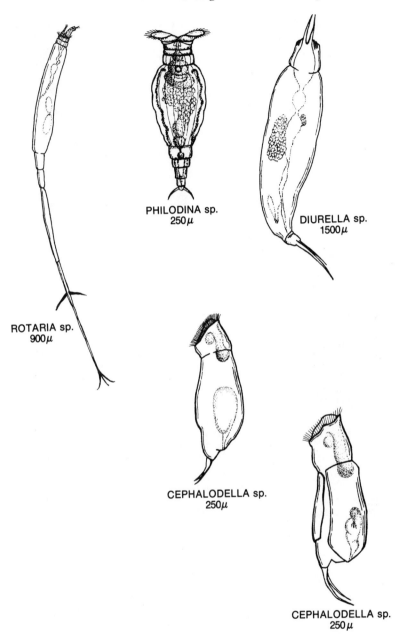

ROTARIA sp.
900μ

PHILODINA sp.
250μ

DIURELLA sp.
1500μ

CEPHALODELLA sp.
250μ

CEPHALODELLA sp.
250μ

A group of typical rotifers. *(Courtesy Xerox Education Publications)*

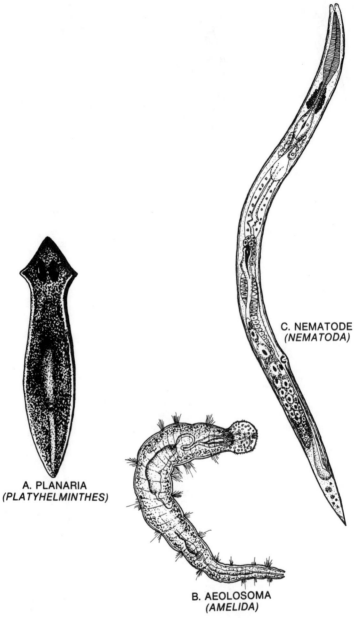

C. NEMATODE
(NEMATODA)

A. PLANARIA
(PLATYHELMINTHES)

B. AEOLOSOMA
(AMELIDA)

From left to right: a flatworm, a segmented worm, a roundworm (nematode). *(Courtesy Xerox Education Publications)*

worms. You might also come across different types of flat-worms. Most of these are big enough to be seen with the unaided eye. If they are in your water sample, you will see them. A well-known and favorite creature among amateur biologists is the planaria worm. This is a black, arrow-shaped worm. It has two black eyespots arranged in a "cross-eyed" pattern.

Crustacea [kruh-STAY-she-uh]: You know what shrimp and lobsters are. Among other things, they are good to eat. The muscles (the part we eat) are inside the shell-like skeleton. You probably know that you have to peel off the outside shell (skeleton) to get at the meat inside. Lobsters, shrimp, and crabs belong to a class of animals called crustaceans. In practically any sample of pond water you are likely to find hundreds of tiny crustaceans—relatives of shrimps and lobsters. These tiny shrimplike creatures are among the most fascinating you are likely to see. They have antennae, many legs, and eyes that are quite obviously eyes. They are sufficiently transparent for you to see the internal parts. One of the more fascinating things you are likely to see in these tiny shrimp is the beating heart. You might also be able to see eggs inside the female. One species of tiny shrimp, cyclops [SIGH-clops] (so called because it has one eye), carries its eggs in little "bags" on the side of the body.

Most of these animals can be seen with the unaided eye; they are generally too large to be viewed with a cover slip on a flat slide. A depression slide or a petroleum jelly well may be needed for these active little animals. A very interesting form of these tiny shrimp is the ostracod. At first you might overlook these animals. They might look like little grains of sand, but a closer look will reveal legs and antennae through that "grain of sand." An ostracod has two shells that almost completely enclose the animal. The tips of the legs might "peek through" the shell at some points.

Some of these tiny shrimp swim rather smoothly through the water, while others move in a jerky fashion. The jerky move-ment shown by some of these animals has led to their being called "water fleas."

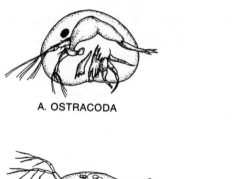

A. OSTRACODA

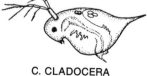

C. CLADOCERA

B. COPEPODA

Representative members of the three orders of tiny crustaceans. *(Courtesy Xerox Education Publications)*

Other pond-water animals: There are many more kinds of tiny pond animals that require a little more effort to collect them then just dipping a jar into the pond. Among the more interesting of these is the hydra, a freshwater relative of jellyfishes. From a fairly clean pond, collect stems of water plants. Be sure that the stems you collect have been under the water. Also, if they are there, collect some of the floating leaves of water lilies. The hydra stick themselves to the stems and to the undersides of the water lily leaves. They might also be found attached to floating sticks and other debris. Put the leaves, stems, et cetera, in a jar of pond water. Transfer all of the materials, water included, to a deep bowl. Keep the bowl in moderate light and temperature of about 20° C (70° F). After a few days, you should see the hydra clinging to the surface of the water. The hydra looks like a stalk to which are attached several tentacles. It's difficult to say how long they are, as they can stretch out their bodies or contract them into a tight little ball. When they are relaxed, they are about a centimeter long. They can stretch out to about 20 millimeters

(3/8 to 3/4 inch). If you focus carefully, you can see the individual cells in the animal's body. After the little animals get used to their new surroundings, they will stretch out and move their tentacles about. It is best to give them a little room on either a depression or a well slide.

If you have any tiny shrimp, you can use them to feed your hydra. Place some hydra in some water with the tiny shrimp. Examine with a low- or medium-power microscope. Very soon the hydra will react to the presence of the tiny shrimp. They will grab them with their tentacles and sting them with some of the many stingers in the tentacles. The hydra then bring the food to the mouth with the tentacles. You can watch the hydra "shoot out" stinging cells from the tentacles by putting a little vinegar in the water on the slide.

Some of the hydras might have little hydras growing out of the sides. That process is known as budding; it is one of the ways hydra reproduce. After the bud gets to be about as big as the parent hydra, it breaks off. Hydra also reproduce by shedding egg and sperm cells into the water. Some of the hydra may be seen to have bumps or ridges along the body. These bumps produce egg or sperm cells.

Plants

Water plants: The variety of water plants is almost endless. One of the more interesting water plants you can observe is more easily "collected" in an aquarium store than in a pond. At the aquarium store ask for a sprig of *Elodea* [ee-low-DEE-ah] (also called anacharis). Be sure to keep the sprig in water. Take off one of the leaves and place it in a drop of water on a slide. A cover slip is optional but should be used if you plan to examine the leaf with high power. This leaf is fairly thick compared to many other things you might look at, so be sure you have enough light. You will also need to focus carefully up and down with the fine adjustment, to see the different levels of the cells.

You should be able to see oval-shaped green objects stream-ing around in a circular pattern in the protoplasm of each cell. The cells are very definitely marked off by the cell walls. The lit-tle green oval objects are the plant's chlorophyll. Each one is called a *chloroplast.* The light and heat from your light source should make the streaming go a little faster after a while. How-ever, the streaming will slow down as the water evaporates.

Other plants: Plants and parts of plants generally found around the house can provide you with some very interesting viewing. You will be surprised to find out how much there is to see in a thinly sliced piece of apple, potato, geranium stem, piece of onion, and other parts of plants. The key to getting good ob-servations is found in the words "thinly sliced." You will remember that words such as thin, thick, heavy, light, far, and so on, are comparative words. You may, for example, think of a po-tato chip as thin. However, compared to the thinness needed for many microscopic examinations, a potato chip is grossly thick.

Cutting thin sections is difficult, but there are ways to do it. You probably don't have a microtome, but you can still get some pretty thin sections. You can, if you want to, make a crude microtome. Go the hardware store and get a large nut and bolt. A bolt with a diameter of about one half inch to one inch should do. The thread should be as fine as you can get. (A nut and bolt with a very coarse thread will not be satisfactory.) The idea of a microtome is that it advances the material to be sliced a tiny bit at a time. You can do pretty much the same thing with the nut and bolt.

To use your homemade microtome, cut and trim a piece of the material you wish to cut (such as a chunk of potato) to fit snugly into the well of the nut. With a sharp knife or other cutting tool, cut the potato so that the edge is flush with the edge of the nut. Now, turn the nut just a tiny bit. Place the knife closely against the edge of the nut and bring it down to cut a slice of the potato. If the slice is as thin as it should be, it will probably stick to the knife. Dip the knife in a small bowl of water, and the slice should come loose and float in the water.

Cut several slices, advancing a little bit with each slice and floating each one in the water. You can then get the slice on a microscope slide by dipping the slide in the water and bringing it under a slice of material. If the sections won't float, place them directly in a drop of water on a slide. Of course, you will need practice before you can get best results. You must be very careful with cutting tools. Avoid holding small pieces of slippery material while attempting to cut slices: the knife could slip and cut you. A good type of knife to use is the type used by hobbyists to cut balsa wood.

The nut-and-bolt microtome can't be used with everything. It will not, for example, be particularly effective for cutting an eight-inch-diameter stem. You could get a whole set of nuts and bolts to accommodate variously sized material. *Histologists,* scientists who study the microscopic structure of living things, go through long, complicated routines to get thin slices and to stain them so that certain parts stand out. For example, pieces of material are embedded in paraffin. The paraffin holds the material so that thin sections can be cut.

Potato: First look at the thin section of potato without staining. After you get the slice of potato on the slide, cover it with a cover slip. Use low power and moderate light to start. Focus up and down carefully with the fine adjustment. With a little practice, you should be able to see the many-sided potato cells. You can get a very definite three-dimensional effect with careful focusing. If you concentrate on one cell, focusing up and down very carefully, you might be able to see all the sides of the cell. After observing the unstained slice, stain a slice with some iodine solution. To do this, put a drop of iodine solution on the slice, then cover with a cover slip. You should be able to see some blue-black spots in the cells. Those dark spots are starch. You may have heard that potatoes are "starchy," and by staining with iodine you can see just how starchy they are. Starch turns a blue-black color in the presence of iodine.

Apples and pears: It might be interesting to compare the microscopic appearance of an apple and a pear. Cut thin sections and mount them on separate slides. Pears on the unripe, hard side are better than soft, ripe pears for this purpose. You may have noticed that when you eat a pear, especially one that is not too ripe, it has a "gritty" feel to it. With the microscope you can see the grainy stuff in the pear that gives it a rough texture. You can also see why an apple feels a good deal smoother in your mouth. Try looking at sections of other fruits and vegetables.

Stems: Stems are the "pipelines" of plants. They carry water and dissolved minerals from the roots to the leaves. They carry food from the leaves to the rest of the plant. Running through the length of the stem are different kinds of tubes that conduct the water and food materials. To get a look at these tubes, you need thin sections of the stem. The easiest kind of section to cut is the cross-section. You get a cross-section by cutting across the stem the short way as though you were cutting slices of salami for a sandwich.

There are three main kinds of plants that have stems with water- and food-conducting tubes in them. These are the ferns, pine trees and similar plants (gymnosperms), and flowering plants. The stems of these plants have their own particular characteristics. The flowering plants are divided into two large subgroups with very long names, but, for now, they can be shortened to *monocot* and *dicot*. Monocots include grasses; grains (grains are really grass) such as corn, wheat, and rice; palm trees; lilies; and orchids. Plants that grow from bulbs, such as gladioli, are monocots. The leaves of monocots are long and pointy, like those of grass.

Most dicots have flat leaves. This group includes practically all the familiar flowering plants — roses, geraniums, peas, beans, and so on — and trees that shed their leaves in the fall. The major difference between monocots and dicots can be seen in the way the stems are put together. The conducting tubes in dicots are arranged in neat circles, while those of monocots are scattered. In woody monocots, such as trees and shrubs, the tubes tend to form circles all the way around the stem. In dicots with softer stems, such as sunflowers, tubes are separate and arranged in a circular pattern. You can tell one kind of plant from another by the arrangement of the tubes in the stem. Try staining the cross-sections. You can try iodine, food coloring, ink, and fabric dyes.

Roots: Cross-sections and long sections of roots can be prepared the same way as outlined for stems. A carrot root is particularly suitable for sectioning. The carrot is rigid enough for cutting and it is large enough to cut safely. A carrot is a dicot, so you will see the conducting vessels arranged in a circle.

Root and leaf hairs: You have probably noticed that the stems and leaves of many plants have hairlike growths on them. These hairs show many interesting shapes and designs. Scrape some of the hairs into a drop of water on a slide. Cover with a cover slip and observe. Be careful with stem and leaf hairs; some are "prickly" and "itchy."

Leaves: To get thin sections of leaves, place the leaf between two thin pieces of balsa wood. Cut through the wood and the leaf. Try to make your leaf section as thin as you possibly can. Put the leaf section in a drop of water on a slide. You might be able to make out definite layers of cells in the leaf section. The top layer is made of closely packed cells (remember that your image is upside down). The cells in this top layer are "up and down" in relation to the rest of the leaf. Under the closely packed cells is a layer of more loosely arranged cells. The bottom layer of cells is made of comparatively small cells. The bottom of the leaf has openings. These openings, called *stomates,* allow water to escape from the leaf and gases to go in and out.

Seeds: A brief look at some kinds of seeds will show you a major difference between monocots and dicots. You may have noticed that seeds of beans (such as lima beans and peas) tend to split into two parts. Each half of the seed is called a *cotyledon* (cotty-leed-uhn). Since there are two of them, these plants are called dicotyledons (dicots). When the seed turns into a very young plant, the cotyledons provide food for the plant until it can grow its own leaves. For that reason, cotyledons are called "seed leaves." If you take a look at a corn seed, you will find that it does not tend to split. That is because the corn seed has only one cotyledon — hence the name for this type of plant is monocotyledon (monocots).

Try taking sections of seeds both the long and the short way. Be particularly careful, especially with corn seeds. Corn seeds are likely to slip out from your fingers. Try holding the seed with a small pair of needlenose pliers. Test the seed sections for the presence of starch with iodine solution.

Flowers: If you pull away the petals and the little green leaflike things (called sepals) from the stem of a flower, you will see the "business part" of the flower. The yellow things inside the flower are the *stamens.* They make the yellow, powdery material called *pollen.* The vase-shaped object is the *pistil.* Try making some cross-sections of the rounded-out part of the pistil at the base. The egg cells that will become seeds are in that part of the pistil. The egg cells won't become seeds until they have combined with the nuclei of pollen grains. Taking a long section of the pistil is difficult. However, if you put some pollen on the top of the pistil and then take a long section, you might be able to see tubes extending from the pollen grains down into the base of the pistil.

The powdery yellow pollen is made up of individual grains. The grains are interesting to observe. Observe pollen grains from different kinds of flowers. Just sprinkle some pollen on a slide. Putting them in a little water under a cover slip might improve the image. Since the pollen grains are round, you will have to focus up and down carefully with the fine adjustment. Cut down the light and you might be able to see the surface features. Each kind of pollen grain has its own arrangement of bumps, ridges, and grooves.

Germinating pollen grains: Pollen grains germinate when they come into contact with a sugary substance on top of the pistil. When the pollen grains germinate, a bulge starts to grow from the grain. This bulge gets longer and becomes a long *pollen tube.*

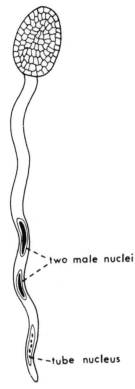

two male nuclei

tube nucleus

A germinating pollen grain.

This tube works its way down through the pistil into the bottom part where the eggs are.

You can "trick" the pollen grains into germinating by putting them in some sugar water. The problem, however, is knowing how strong to make the sugar water. You have to find out the right strength of sugar water by experimenting. For example, you could start with one teaspoon of sugar in a cup (or 250 milliliters) of water. Put a small drop of the sugar water on a slide, sprinkle some pollen into the water, and cover with a cover slip. Make sure the layer of water under the cover slip is thin. The cover slip should not be floating on the water. Keep the slide warm at about 22° C (75° F). (You can warm the slide *slightly* in an oven.) Check on the slide every fifteen minutes or so. You will probably need medium to high power to see the pollen tubes. If, after a few hours, no pollen tubes have formed, try a different concentration of sugar water. Keep records of the kinds of pollen and the concentrations of sugar water you use.

Onion cells: You don't have to do any thin-sectioning to observe the cells of an onion. Cut an onion into wedges (eighths are fine). Take one of the curved pieces of onion and snap it in two. You will see a thin, almost transparent, membrane between the onion leaves. With the help of a pair of tweezers, pull off a small piece of this membrane and put it in a drop of water on a slide. Use pins, needles, or some other sharp instrument to get the onion membrane to lie as flat as possible in the drop of water. Cover with a cover slip. Examine first under low power. You should see onion cells arranged in fairly neat columns. They look somewhat like paving blocks. You should be able to pick out the cell walls. The space inside the cell walls looks empty, but it is filled with an oily fluid. That oily fluid is what gives onions their flavor and smell. It is also what can make you cry when you peel and cut an onion.

After you observe the unstained cells, try staining them. You might want to try a different way of getting stain on the specimen. Put a drop of stain (such as iodine solution) on one side of the cover slip. Be sure the drop of stain is in contact with the cover slip. Then touch a small piece of paper toweling to the other side. The paper toweling should draw the water out from under the cover slip, and the stain liquid should move in under the cover slip.

After staining, you should be able to see the nucleus in each cell. The nucleus, a roundish object, will be stained a deep brown. The nucleus of onion cells is generally not in the center of the cell. In most of the cells the nucleus will be nearly in contact with the *cell wall*. Plant cells have a cell wall, while animal cells do not. If you focus carefully with a higher power, you might be able to see that the cell wall is a double wall. Animal cells have what is called a cell membrane. The cell wall of plants is made of a material called *cellulose*. It is what gives plants their rigidity. Wood is all cellulose. It is the cell walls of dead cells. A thin section through a woody stem will show the "open" cells of wood. These cells conduct water in woody plants. Wood can be a bit difficult to cut in thin sections. However, you can see similar cells in a thinly cut piece of cork. If you do examine cork, you will be repeating the experiments of Robert Hooke, a pioneer microscope maker.

Fungi: Fungi [FUN-jeye] is the plural of the word fungus [FUN-gus]. Fungi are everywhere. Mushrooms are fungi, as are bread mold, mildew, and yeast. Fungi grow in many different forms and shapes. Mushrooms, for example, are only one part of the fungus. Most of it is underground, growing in a tangled mass of threadlike filaments called mycelium [my-SEE-lee-um]. The mushrooms are the part of the fungus that reproduce more fungi. Sometimes you may have seen a black or brown powder coming out a wild mushroom. That black powder is *spores*. A spore is something like a seed. If a spore lands in the right place and has good growing conditions, it will grow into a new fungus.

Bread mold: The fungus called bread mold grows on many things besides bread. It is frequently seen on jams and jellies and growing on fruits and vegetables. If you can't find any bread mold, you can grow some yourself. Sprinkle some dust on a piece of moist bread — not sopping wet, just moist. Line a plastic bag (medium size) with moist paper toweling. Put the slice of bread in the bag between the paper towels. Keep the bag in the dark, in a moderately warm place (about 80° F; 27° C), for about a week. You should get all kinds of mold on the bread. If you don't want to use bread, you can use a piece of fruit.

The first mold that usually appears on the bread is the common bread mold called *Rhizopus* [RYE-zuh-pus]. Other molds such as *Penicillium* [pen-uh-SILL-ee-um] and *Aspergillus* [ass-per-JILL-us] grow after a while.

To examine the mold, pick up a bit of it with a pair of tweezers and put it in a drop of water on a slide. Add a cover slip. You will be able to see the strands of mycelium. You might also see some spherical black objects attached to stalks of mycelium. The black spheres are called sporangia [spoh-RANDGE-ee-uh]. They contain spores and are like the "mushrooms" of the mold.

The spores of *Aspergillus* grow in clusterlike arrangements. Spores of *Penicillium* grow on stalked branches of myecelium.

Yeast: Here is a fungus you can "collect" at the supermarket. To examine individual yeast cells, take a small pinch of cake yeast or just a bit of dry yeast and mix it with a little water. Stir it up well. Put a drop of the yeast-water suspension on a slide, add a cover slip, and examine. Use a low power first, and then advance to higher powers.

Yeast cells reproduce by forming buds. These buds pinch off to become new cells. Budding can be encouraged by making a yeast-cell suspension in sugar water. Make a 5 percent solution by dissolving five grams of sugar in 100 milliliters of water. The sugar water should be at about room temperature. Examine a drop of the yeast suspension every fifteen minutes or so. Buds appear as little bulges on the cells. Sometimes, buds form on buds and you can get "chains" of yeast cells. You will notice that the sugar water-yeast suspension is bubbly. The bubbling comes from carbon dioxide which is formed by the action of the yeast on the sugar.

Other fungi: Molds, mildews, and other fungi are everywhere. Scrape off a little from whatever it is growing on, and examine it in a drop of water on a slide.

Mosses and ferns: Mosses grow in damp woods. They are familiar plants, so familiar that most of us don't ever take the time to really look at them. You can really take a close look at them with your microscope. The basic idea is to put the material in a drop of water and cover with a cover slip. If you have some glycerine, try putting the moss leaf in a drop of that instead of water. The glycerine will help to bring out some of the features of the leaf. You should be able to see the individual cells. Try to

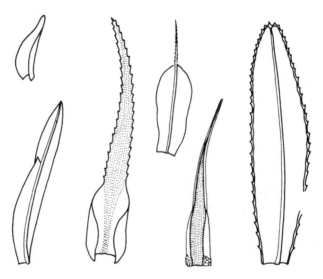

Several types of moss leaves.

examine as many different kinds of moss leaves as you can. They come in many different interesting shapes and designs.

If you look closely at moss, you will find slender, tiny, brownish stalks growing from the green mat of the moss. These are sporangia, the spore-producing organs of the moss. The spores are produced in the little cylinderlike structure at the top of the stalk. Examine a few of these cylinders on a dry slide without a cover slip. Use the lowest power. If you have a dissecting microscope, you will find that it is excellent for examining the sporangia. Examine as many different kinds of these as you can find. Sporangia have little "caps." You will be amazed at the many weird shapes of these caps. Many of them have what can be described as "teeth" forming a ring around the top. These teeth respond to changes in humidity by moving back and forth. You might be able to see this movement by breathing on them while looking at them with your microscope.

Crush one of the sporangia in a drop of water on a slide. Add a cover slip. You will see spores, cells, and other structures.

If you take a look at the underside of fern leaves you are likely to find brownish to black spots. Collect a few of the leaves that have these brown spots on them. The spots are called sori (SORE-eye). They produce spores which can grow into new fern plants. Crush some of the sori in a drop of water on a slide and examine the spores. The spores do not grow directly into the familiar green fern plants. They grow into a tiny, heart-shaped flat plant called a *prothallus*. If you collect some of the soil from under a fern plant that has sori, you might be able to collect some of these prothalli. They are about an eighth of an inch in size and can be seen with the unaided eye. A prothallus produces a new fern plant through sexual reproduction—the fertilization of an egg cell by a sperm cell.

Lichens: Lichens are found growing on rocks, trees, sides of buildings, gravestones, and just about everywhere. A lichen is a combination of a fungus and an alga. The fungus and lichen live together in what is called *mutualism*. The algae provide food for the fungus, and the fungus provides a "house" for the algae. Lichens occur in many different varieties. Some are just flat, greenish or grayish growths on rocks. Others have brightly colored "fruiting bodies." To collect lichens, scrape the growths off trees and whatever they are growing on and carry them home in plastic bags. Many lichens are hard and difficult to crush for examination with a microscope. Soaking the bits of lichen in water for a few hours will help to soften them. Cut, shred, or tear the material, and mount it in water on a slide. Mounting in glycerin will help to bring out some of the features.

Insects

You will certainly have no problem finding insects. Some insects are small enough to be examined whole with a compound microscope. But a dissecting microscope is better for examining whole larger insects. You can put an entire ant, mosquito, gnat, or other small insect on a slide. However, they must be dead. When they are alive, they are not going to stand still just so you can look at them. A microscope will show you there is much more to an insect than you might have believed.

The "stinger," or biting parts, of a mosquito show up well. Actually, the mosquito does not bite in the true sense of the word. It punctures the skin with its needlelike mouth part, and drinks blood like soda pop through a straw. The biting part is easy to see. Through the microscope, it appears to be a very long, transparent tube coming out of the head.

Legs and wings are very interesting to look at. A dead fly, for example, should not be too difficult to obtain. Look at its parts separately. Examining the legs will show you why flies can walk up walls and stand upside down on the ceiling. You will find the legs have many hairs, tufts, and bristles. Insect wings fascinated early microscope makers, such as Robert Hooke, and they can fascinate you, too. Put a fly's wing on a slide, and examine it under different intensities of light. You will see different patterns of color with each change of light.

Nonliving Material

There is practically no limit to what you can look at with your microscope. Ordinary stuff lying around the house can become beautiful, spectacular sights when examined with microscope.

Crystals can provide you with some breathtaking beauty. There are crystals all over your house, whether you know it or not. There is most certainly some salt in the house. Put a few grains — that is, crystals — of salt on a microscope slide. Examine them with reduced light and you will think you are looking at diamonds. You can do the same with sugar. Look at some sugar and salt crystals together. You should look around for some other crystals in the house. There might be some citric acid (sour salt) in the spice cabinet, and there might also be some copper sulfate (blue vitriol) around.

Paper: Examine different kinds of paper. Just put a piece of paper on a slide, and put a cover slip on it to hold it down. You can do without the cover slip, but there's a chance that your breathing might blow the piece of paper away. Look at different qualities of paper. The difference between newsprint and high-quality glossy paper is obvious. Don't forget to look at printed letters. That smooth printed letter on the page doesn't look so smooth through the microscope.

Cloth: Most cloth allows enough light to pass through to make observation with your microscope possible. Usually, low powers give you a better view of how the cloth is put together. Look at different kinds of cloth. Compare natural fibers, such as cotton and wool, with synthetic materials, such as nylon and polyester. You will be able to see the fibers in white cloth more clearly than you can in dyed cloth. However, you should also examine colored cloth to see how the fibers take up the dye. Frequently, you can examine cloth without a slide. Just stretch the cloth tightly over the stage of your microscope. Be sure that the part of the cloth over the hole in the stage is pulled tightly.

Other observations:

Put a color photographic slide on the stage and examine it with low power. You can also look at movie film. Compare slides made from different brands of film. See if one brand is "grainier" than another.

Tips of needles and pins: Place the point on the slide so that the tip is over the hole in the stage. You will be surprised at just how rough "sharp" can be.

Phonograph records: If you have a phonograph record made of transparent material, you can examine the grooves. You would need a dissecting microscope to examine the grooves in an opaque (not transparent) record. You could, however, try putting a strong light source over the microscope stage. You would have to experiment to find the best angle for directing the light.

Dust: Just leave a slide in a dusty place for a few hours. Put the slide on your microscope, and look.

Microscope art: Here is one suggestion. Smear some egg white on a slide. Allow it to dry. Dip the slide in some food coloring for a minute or two. Take it out and allow it to dry. Wipe the side of the slide that does not have the egg white on it. Then look at the slide. Many people say that the result is as good as many kinds of "abstract art" found in museums. Try different colors on the same slide. You can also try other clear substances, such as airplane glue and paints.

Resources

Ask any amateur or professional astronomer or microscopist if he or she knows all there is to know about microscopes and telescopes and what can be done with them, and you will get an emphatic "no" for an answer. There is always more to learn, and that is good. For the more there is to learn, the less likely you are to get bored. There is certainly a lot of good information in the books and magazines listed here, but the best source of information is people who are experienced in using microscopes and telescopes. Profiting from the experience of others is why people with similar interests get together to form clubs and organizations.

There are many amateur astronomical societies in the United States and Canada. Unfortunately, the same thing cannot be said for societies of amateur microscopists. There are amateur astronomical societies in every state, and there is probably one not very far from you. However, astronomical societies are not very noticeable. They do not demonstrate, hold noisy rallies, dress in funny costumes, or do anything else that might attract attention. Therefore, your local or nearby astronomical society may be difficult to find. One way to find it is to ask at the astronomy department of a nearby college. Someone there will probably know.

If there is no astronomical society near you, you might try starting one yourself. It's not easy, but the results might be worth the effort. You could get help from a science teacher in a high school or college. Many schools have science clubs of one kind or another, and astronomy clubs sometimes branch off from these.

Trying to get a microscope club going would probably be more difficult than starting an astronomy club. Microscopy is not the kind of activity that usually lends itself to togetherness. It is possible, however. A good place to start is in a school. With the help of a biology teacher, find other people who are also interested in microscopy. You can hold regular meetings during which you can swap ideas or perhaps invite a guest speaker.

MAGAZINES

Sky and Telescope. Cambridge, Massachusetts: Sky Publishing Company.

Science and Children. Washington, D.C.: National Science Teachers Association.

BOOKS: TELESCOPES

Alter, G., et al., eds., *Catalogue of Star Clusters and Associations,* 2nd ed. New York: Adler.

Amateur Astronomers Handbook, The, New York: Crowell, 1974.

Baker, R., *When the Stars Come Out.* New York: Viking, 1975.

Boss, Benjamin, *General Catalogue of 33,342 Stars for the Epoch 1950.* Washington, D.C.: Carnegie Institute of Washington, Department of Meridian Astronomy.

Brown, Peter L., *Star and Planet Spotting.* London: Bladford Press, 1974.

Callaway, M., *Atlas of the Moon.* New York: Macmillan, 1964.

Cleminshaw, C. H., *The Beginner's Guide to the Skies.* New York: Crowell, 1977.

Cooper, Joseph P., *Photography Through Monoculars, Binoculars, and Telescopes.* Garden City, N.Y.: AmPhoto.

Lapidus, Saul, *The Telescope Catalog of Catalogs.* New York: McKay, 1978.

Menzel, Donald H., *A Field Guide to Stars and Planets.* Boston: Houghton Mifflin,

Moore, Patrick, *Astronomical Telescopes and Observatories for Amateurs.* New York, N.Y.: Norton, 1973

Muirden, J., *Beginner's Guide to Astronomical Telescope Making.* Levittown, N.Y.: Transatlantic, 1976.

Neale, H., *Standard Handbook for Telescope Making.* New York: Crowell, 1959.

Page, T., and Page, L., *Telescopes: How to Make and Use Them* (Sky and Telescope Library of Astronomy). New York: Macmillan, 1966.

Papadopolous, C., *Photographic Star Atlas, vol. 3, Northern Stars.* New York: Pergamon, 1978.

Polgern, J., and Polgern, C., *The Stars Tonight.* New York: Harper and Row,

Raphael, A., *Raphael's Astro Ephemeris.* Cedar Knolls, N.J.: Wehman, (latest year).

United States Naval Observatory, Nautical Almanac Office, *The American Ephemeris and Nautical Almanac.* Washington, D.C.: U. S. Government Printing Office (annually).

Zdenek, Kopal, *A New Photographic Atlas of the Moon.* New York: Taplinger, 1971.

Zim, H., *stars* (Golden Guide Series). New York: Western.

BOOKS: MICROSCOPES

Beeler, Nelson, and Branley, F., *Experiments with a Microscope.* New York: Crowell, 1957.

Burrells, W., *Microscopic Technique.* New York: Halsted, 1978.

Clark, G. L., ed., *Encyclopedia of Microscopy.* New York: Reinhold, 1961.

Gray, Peter, *Encyclopedia of Microscopy and Micro-Technique.* New York: Van Nostrand-Reinhold, 1973.

——— *Handbook of Basic Microtechnique.* New York: McGraw-Hill, 1964.

Gurr, E., *Encyclopedia of Microscope Stains.* Baltimore: Williams and Wilkins, 1961.

Headstrom, Rachel, *Adventures with a Microscope.* New York: Dover.

Humason, Gretchen, *Animal Tissue Technique.* San Francisco: Freeman, 1979.

Humphreys, Donald W., *What's That Little Thing in the Water?* Columbus, Ohio: Xerox Education Publication, 1977.

Jahn, T., and Jahn, F., *How to Know the Protozoa.* Dubuque, Iowa: William C. Brown, 1949.

Johansen, Donald, *Plant Microtechnique.* New York: McGraw-Hill,

Klein, Aaron E., *Seedlings and Soil.* New York: Doubleday, 1973.

——— *The Electron Microscope.* New York: McGraw-Hill, 1974.

McClung, C. D., and Jones, R., eds., *Handbook of Microscopical Technique for Workers in Animal and Plant Tissue,* 3rd ed. New York: Harper and Row.

Morholt, E., Brandwein, P., and Alexander, Joseph, *A Sourcebook for the Biological Sciences.* New York: Harcourt, Brace, Jovanovich, 1972.

Needham, George H., *The Microscope: A Practical Guide.* Springfield, Illinois: Charles C. Thomas Co., 1968.

Needham, J., and Raul, R., *A Guide to the Study of Freshwater Biology.* San Francisco: Holden-Day, 1962.

Pennak, R. W., *Freshwater Invertebrates of the United States.* New York: Ronald Press, 1953.

Sass, John E., *Botanical Microtechnique.* Ames, Iowa: Iowa State University Press, 1958.

Ward, H. G., and Whipple, G. C., *Freshwater Biology.* New York: John Wiley and Sons, 1959.

COMPANIES THAT SELL TELESCOPES, MICROSCOPES, AND MATERIALS AND PARTS FOR MAKING TELESCOPES

American Optical Corporation
Buffalo, New York 14215
Microscopes and Microscope Accessories.

Bausch and Lomb
Optical Products Division
1400 North Goodman Street
Rochester, New York 14602
Microscopes and Accessories, Terrestrial Telescopes.

Celestron International
2835 Columbia Street
Torrance, California 90503
Cassegrain and Maksutov Reflecting Telescopes and Accessories.

Edmund Scientific Company
101 East Gloucester Pike
Barrington, New Jersey 08007
Microscopes, Telescopes, Parts and Supplies for Making Telescopes. (Including Mirror-grinding Kits), General Scientific Supplies.

Meade Instruments Corporation
721 West 16th Street
Costa Mesa, California 92627
Telescopes and Parts for Assembling Telescopes.

Olympus Corporation of America
4 Nevada Drive
New Hyde Park, New York 11040
Microscopes and Accessories.

Swift Instruments Inc.
952 Dorchester Avenue
Boston, Massachusetts 02125
Microscopes, Telescopes, Binoculars, and Accessories.

Tasco Sales Inc.
1075 N.W. 71st Street
Miami, Florida 33138
Microscopes, Telescopes, Binoculars, and Accessories.

Unitron Instruments Inc.
101 Crossways Park West
Woodbury, New York 11797
Microscopes, Telescopes, and Accessories.

About the Author

AARON E. KLEIN was born in Atlanta, Georgia, and educated in the public schools of Georgia and Connecticut and the universities of Pennsylvania, Bridgeport, Yale, and Wesleyan. For over ten years he taught biology in secondary schools and colleges. He is now a freelance science writer and author of many science books for young readers. Mr. Klein's books for Doubleday include *Beyond Time and Matter, The Hidden Contributors, Science and the Supernatural, Threads of Life, You and Your Body,* and *Mind Trips.*

INDEX